Mighty Manifestations

Reinhard Bonnke

D0311528

CREATION HOUSE

BOOKS ABOUT SPIRIT-LED LIVING

ORLANDO, FLORIDA

Creation House
Strang Communications Company
600 Rinehart Road
Lake Mary, FL 32746
1-800-599-5750

First published by Kingsway Publications, Eastbourne, 1994

Cover photograph: Tony Stone Images, London

Cover Concept: Vanessa Birkbeck

Contents

Introduction

Multitudes have been baptized in the Holy Spirit this century; many have receivedthe baptism of the Holy Spirit in our own gospel crusades. We regularly witness many mighty manifestations of the power and love of God.

This book, *Mighty Manifestations,* is the result of a desire to explain to others the understanding my associates and I have gained from these events in which we have been so deeply involved. (To date, the only other material we have published about the working of the Holy Spirit was a booklet about the baptism of the Holy Spirit.)

My final authority has been Scripture. Certainly experience has helped me grasp the things of the Spirit, but as Peter wrote, God "has given to us all things that pertain to life and godliness" (2 Pet. 1:3). Scripture validates experience.

It became obvious to me that I must record the understanding we have of the things of the Spirit and show that my conclusions were arrived at through the Word, illuminated by what I have seen. I enlisted George Canty to help in the writing. Our reason for recording this is that there are many books in print today presenting many alternative views. Variations are sure to exist unless a standard authority is accepted and agreed upon to judge all such teachings. Experience itself varies, but the Scriptures do not. There is a natural public appetite to hear things God has done and a strong tendency to draw teaching primarily from experience; the Word is regarded only as a secondary backup, if used at all.

This "anecdote theology" is not new. There are theories of revival, for example, which have been openly claimed as being based purely on studies of what has happened in the past. I was concerned about this approach as I viewed the tremendous burst of divine revival phenomena today. I decided that, for us, our grounds must be the Word. And that is where we stand. Over the months that it took to put this book together our entire "pneumatology" (the things of the Spirit) had to be subject to the judgment of what the Word says. This was wholesome discipline. We have made the study as thorough and clear as possible, to the best of our ability.

Experience must be challenged by Scripture; experience must not challenge Scripture nor adapt Scripture to what "happens to happen." Nevertheless, readers will see that we do illustrate our teaching with things God has been doing in our evangelistic crusades.

Of course, among Christians who pray for and support the nation-shaking campaigns of Christ for All Nations there is obviously a considerable variety of viewpoints on many doctrines, including that of the Holy Spirit. I offer this exposition of the

Word as a contribution to the understanding of the work of the Holy Spirit.

When it comes to the great and most important interest of evangelism, I work with people of many different spiritual affirmations. Christ for All Nations is an evangelist-servant to the churches wherever they labor and whatever their witness or emphasis. Through their constant help and in the power of the Spirit, we have been privileged to bring entire nations face-to-face personally with the gospel of Christ crucified and have thoroughly checked the outcome by the Word.

This book is our practical "thank you" for the wonderful support and encouragement of countless thousands. It is meant to throw light on the beliefs which stimulate our operations in the harvest field. Of course, it makes no pretense of being an academic treatise, but the work of countless scholars has influenced it. Nor is it a rehash of current popular teaching.

I have not written merely to sell a book and repeat what has been said before without examination. Others will certainly have seen and said things contained in this book, but everything here has come from a fresh examination of the Word. It is freshly minted coinage representing an original and independent perusal of Scripture, avoiding speculation. That is my guiding principle. My purpose is to render guidance in the midst of the present global outpouring of the Spirit and the acres of print which it inspires daily.

Two lifetimes of accumulated knowledge, worldwide experience and practice are combined here for the benefit of readers: my own years of mass evangelism and also those of the pioneer evangelist/writer George Canty. He has been actively involved with the whole sweep of what the Holy Spirit has been doing in this century of charismatic revival. His personal acquaintance with leaders and early Pentecostal pioneers around the globe combined with his vast writing experience in history, Scripture and theology have provided him with a great deal of insight few others can claim to contribute to a book like this.

When we speak of the Spirit, some matters are profound. One of the main problems has been to analyze and express them carefully in language which neither insults anybody's intelligence nor presumes upon previous knowledge. I have striven for simplicity without being simplistic. The least or best informed should be able to appreciate these studies.

The book is divided into two parts. Part 1 takes a careful look at what the Scripture teaches about the anointing and gifts of the Holy Spirit in general. Part 2 looks at the specific gifts listed by the apostle Paul in 1 Corinthians 12.

May the Holy Spirit add His illumination to these pages — for the glory of God.

Reinhard Bonnke
Frankfurt, 1994

Part One

1

THREE PILLARS OF WISDOM

God uses manpower. Man needs God's power. God works when people work. Those propositions are the three pillars of wisdom for this book.

Power! That is the essence of the gospel. A powerless gospel preacher is like an unwashed soap salesman. Singing "There is power, power, wonder-working power in the precious blood of the Lamb" and then having to fast and pray for a month to get power does not add up.

At the beginning of my Christian life I had an experience of the coming of the Holy Spirit into my life which I believe was as great as that of any disciple on the day of Pentecost. It seemed to me that the God who fills heaven and earth crowded into my soul.

Peter managed to stand up and preach, but the physical effects of my baptism in the Spirit would certainly have been too much for me to stand and preach immediately, as tremendous as my empowering was for later service.

Many write about their marvelous experiences. Purely as a matter of interest I will tell you how it happened to me, but I ought to say that nobody should think that God ever gives the Spirit in exactly the same way to everyone. It happened like this.

I was a boy of eleven in Germany when my father told me about special prayer meetings for the baptism in the Holy Spirit. Ever eager for the things of God I begged him to take me along. Just one year earlier the Lord had called me to someday preach the gospel in Africa — and I knew I needed the power of the Holy Spirit to do it. A missionary from Finland was visiting the church, and he explained the truth of the baptism in the Holy Spirit. We had just knelt down when the power of God began to pour into and over me. Joy unspeakable filled my heart, and I began to speak in other languages as the Spirit gave me utterance. It was like a heavenly fountain opening up within me; it is still flowing today.

Soon after this I was in a service which my father was leading (with a watchful eye on his son, Reinhard) in a church in North Germany. There was nothing very wrong I could do or wanted to do. I had really found Jesus and wanted to be a preacher/missionary.

Then I began to get an impulse during prayer to do something I thought my father would not like. For no reason at all I could not stop thinking about a woman sitting on the opposite side of the church. I tried to be good, but this feeling grew stronger and stronger. It wasn't just in my head. It seemed to be all over me. I tingled with this feeling more and more, like steadily increasing voltage. I tried to push it out of my mind, but the tingling current became stronger.

I would have to do it. But what would she say, and what would Father do? So I crouched down behind the seats and step-by-step moved across to her. Then I said, "I want to pray for you."

She looked at me and said, "All right — pray for me!" I put my hand on this grown woman, and something happened. The current in my body seemed to jolt right out into her.

At that point, Father couldn't help but notice. As the people in the service were still kneeling in prayer, he asked, "Reinhard, what are you doing?"

The lady answered for me. "Reinhard put his hand on me, and I felt the power of the Lord go through me, and look! I am well! I am healed!"

At that time I did not know the spiritual principles behind this healing. I did not know then that if we are obedient there is enough power from God. I still had to learn that lesson and many like it. Many books tell us about authors' lives and their awe-inspiring visitations and revelations. They are exciting but often leave folks feeling downcast because they have had nothing like it. They think they must be inferior to these God-used people.

In this book I want you to know the truth about the Holy Spirit. It will amount to a great revelation to your heart and will show you what you can be in God. It is for all Christian workers, not only for those who happen to have had some rare and fantastic moments. Many people, I am certain, will be like new people when they have finished reading these chapters.

To unfold the three principles named above I shall have to begin with the basics. Millions of sermons are preached and heard by hundreds of millions of people. But the effect is not so great. Preachers say, "The people don't do what I say." That is it, of course. Of all those who listen, how many feel like exerting themselves, putting themselves out to serve the Lord? Are the rest content only to sing, worship and enjoy a good sermon? Take this book, for example. I hope that many will enjoy and profit from it. But it is those who are "doers…and not hearers only" (James 1:22) who will really share the good things that I want to share. I am not passing on mere knowledge, but trying to lead everybody into the dynamic power and blessing of God.

Let me encourage you first. You can be absolutely sure that God has something for you to do now and a special privileged place in which to put you. You are perhaps already there but don't realize it. Many think that God has some great thing for them to do — one day. Perhaps He has, but what you are doing now is important, too, if you are obeying Him. There's a job to suit you and a job for which you are being prepared. If you think you are not in on these things, it isn't true. Don't deprive yourself of your right and proper place in the glorious scheme of God as set out in this book.

Once you realize that first point, that God uses manpower, you can move on. If God wants you to do something He will give you the ability to do it. Very likely it may stretch you beyond what you have done before. He wants you to grow. Whatever lies before you, God put it there. You can move mountains. Say this to yourself: "God means me to be more than I thought I was." Don't measure what you should do by your gift; measure the gift by what you should do. It will match. God is a God who specializes in the impossible. He thinks only in terms of the impossible. He wants this fact to show in the lives of those who belong to Him. He commands the impossible — and then makes it possible — to His glory.

This book will reveal, page by page, the ways to His power.

Perhaps you wonder why God wants us to do anything at all when He has all power. It is because He loves us and He likes to share His pleasures and joys with us. That is His grand design. You may feel you are a very small instrument, but each of us is vital in the full orchestration. The Lord of all the earth has big things in mind, and they call for millions of helpers with varied gifts and capabilities. We are "vessels" so that "the power may be of God and not of us," as Paul said in 2 Corinthians 4:7.

Starting from the small incident I described above, I have learned that "I can do all things through Christ who strengthens me" (Phil. 4:13). As this book goes to print, I am working to put a gospel booklet into every residence in the British Isles. Obviously no man could do this alone unless he were a multimillionaire, but I began this commission with no funds. In Christ we have the resources of God.

To fulfill God's purpose we should think of ourselves as humble conduits for His Word and Spirit to flow through. A copper pipe can't boast of the water that flows through it to the tap in our homes. We are to let the living waters flow — and just stay unblocked. Whatever gifts or talents we lay at His feet, the Master can use them all. They become accessory parts, shaping the conduit through which God does what He wants.

This is a lesson we must learn well; we must take it deep into our hearts as the foundation for everything else we learn or do.

God has given me my job. Many times I've been asked, "When did you begin to see miracles in your ministry?" "Why do so many turn to Christ when you preach?" The answer is found in what I have just said — God gives us the power to do what He commands. That power comes through the baptism with the Holy Spirit.

I experienced that wonderful baptism, and it has stayed with me, charging and surging within me. I spoke with tongues also, and it was such a marvelous thing to me that I've never doubted since that miracles are for today. Of course, I had faith before. The Word itself has always stirred my faith. Then, when the promise of the Spirit was fulfilled for me — and became an ongoing constant filling — the whole experience boosted my faith like supercharging a car engine. The Bible confirmed what was happening.

When the Spirit Comes

Next I want you to ponder a well-known promise. Let me write out what it really says. You may be too familiar with it and have lost sight of its tremendous wonder, for it is one of the most impossible and fantastic expectations that any person could ever entertain.

> You will be baptized with the Holy Spirit...you will receive power when the Holy Spirit comes on you (Acts 1:5, 8, NIV).

Could it really happen in the twentieth century? Well, it did for me. I can't think of anything more wonderful for human beings than that. It means being filled with God. It isn't "getting high" on God, a sort of euphoric, giddy happiness without substance. The Holy Spirit is not a super drug, tranquilizer or stimulant. He doesn't come to give us an emotional "trip," but, make no mistake about it, His presence is heart-moving. Life is tough. God sends His power to people in tough situations. He is the original life force meant for us all.

Over the years I have come to understand more and more. Fresh enlightenment has burst upon me. It is all so wonderful. God wants me to share it with the whole world in my preaching and now especially in this book.

Christianity: What Is It?

Did you know that when people talk of Christianity as a world religion they are quite wrong? A religion is a system, and Jesus left no system. Christianity is more than just a faith to be believed. Real Christianity is actually divine power in action. Christian truth can't just be written down like so many facts or definitions. Christian truth is alive. You can't draw a picture of a man and say, "That's him!" You can't write Christianity down and say, "That's it!" It is a living entity. The breath of God animates the gospel, or it is a dead body of truth instead of living truth. Jesus said, "I am the way, the truth, and the life" (John 14:6). That is how I know it and how I preach it. Who wouldn't want to preach a gospel like that?

Now let us try to define Christianity with an up-to-date definition as charismatic Pentecostals understand it: It is the Holy Spirit in action making the Word of God happen. We must be able to show people that the gospel is what it claims to be. When a champion athlete stands on the track, we don't need to argue to prove he is world-class. Just fire the starting pistol! That is what I do; the gospel of Christ is alive, so I go into a stadium and let the gospel do its own thing. Everybody can see it is alive. That is what the Holy Spirit does.

Powers of a New Order

I have seen countless mighty wonders and unclean spirits cast out by the finger of God. Christ explained it. "If I cast out demons with the finger of God, surely the kingdom of God has come upon you" (Luke 11:20).

We must look carefully at that explanation. The kingdom — what is it? If we are to catch the real secret of the faith we must understand the kingdom. Jesus talked about it all the time. We only need to consider it from one angle at this point.

We have had different historical ages — the Stone Age, the

Dark Ages and so on. These time periods were given special names to show their main features. We also have the Christian age. This year is A.D. 1994 — *Anno Domini*, in the year of the Lord. Is it just another division of history? No. This age is unique. During the Christian age another age also broke in — the kingdom of God. Jesus began to preach, "Repent, for the kingdom of God is at hand" (Matt. 4:17).

The kingdom is the realm of God in which God's power is supreme. When Christ came He introduced the activity of God the Holy Spirit into our mundane affairs. It was a new resource, not physical power like water, wind or nuclear energy; these are all part of the natural world. This was the power of a world with laws far above the laws of nature.

Read this sentence carefully: In the beginning God made this world by the powers of another world. In Christ Jesus He re-introduced the powers of that creative world into the earthly scene. That is the kingdom of God.

I will explain more in chapter 2, but we should grasp now that our world has been invaded, and the authority of the kingdom of God has drawn near to us. It is a superior order, a miracle order that overarches the natural or scientific order. Higher laws can overrule the physical laws. The spiritual can overrule the material. That happens in the baptism of the Holy Spirit and when His gifts operate.

John 1:1-3 says that all things were made by the Word; that is, by the Son of God, "the Word became flesh" (John 1:14). He who is the source of everything we see — He Himself came into His own creation, the One who "came down from heaven," as He said (John 6:38, KJV). That statement "came down from heaven" is very important. It means that He became the bridge reaching from the higher, invisible world to the visible. In John 1:51 Jesus portrays Himself as a Jacob's ladder set up between heaven and earth.

There are two orders, with their own forces or powers. Jesus is the link between them, the heavenly and the earthly order. The power of heaven is the creative power of God by which the earth was made. Through Christ — the link with heaven — things are possible on earth which were not possible before Christ came. He is called "the new and living way" (Heb. 10:20). Through Jesus Christ, by the Holy Spirit, commerce has begun between earth and heaven. The angels of God are coming and going.

Through the breaking in of Christ into our world, God can exercise His will here — through our prayers. It is a case, as we said, of God's wanting manpower and our needing God's power, for Jesus taught us to pray, "Your will be done on earth as it is in heaven" (Matt. 6:10). He has not shut Himself out of any part of His universe. He is Lord. He applies greater forces, and the natural laws obey by the Spirit of God. We call that a miracle. This age is a new dispensation. God is dealing with us in a new way. There is, of course, a grand purpose behind it. The object is not to pull off a few sensational wonders, like stage tricks, but the redemption of the world.

If you have ever thought about it, every time you move, you bring natural laws under your authority. Left to nature, rocks would not fly, but we human beings introduce a higher law — that of our will. We can throw rocks and make them fly. We are not the slaves of the laws of nature; they are our slaves. We can use the scientific laws to leave this planet altogether. We can move into a state of weightlessness or even fly to the moon.

When people say that miracles are contrary to the laws of nature, they completely ignore the fact that where there is a superior will and superior power — with man as well as omnipotent God — all the laws of nature can be overridden. The difficulty arises when people don't believe in God. Bring God into it, and nothing is impossible. And that is what has happened — the kingdom of God is among us; therefore, devils are cast out, the sick are healed, and we speak with tongues.

There is another fact to be faced. What are human beings? We are both flesh and spirit. God linked us to two worlds, the earthly and the spiritual. By our five senses we are aware of this world, and by our spirits we sense the nonphysical world — and, on occasions, fear it.

But something has gone wrong. A great calamity has befallen us; sin has almost destroyed the link between body and spirit. After the fall of Adam, only occasional flashes of the supernatural were seen until Jesus came. Only a breakthrough now and then is recorded in the Old Testament. Sometimes God exercised His sovereignty and initiated a spate of wonders, as He did with Moses and the Elijah/Elisha ministry. God's power and His authority were rarely seen directly.

Then a radical change came about. Christ's marvelous coming, God in the flesh, opened up the resources of creative power. He was, and is, Lord of all things. He announced it Himself saying, "The kingdom of God is at hand" (Mark 1:14).

At this point we come to the phrase "born again" (John 3:3). One of the possibilities Christ opened up for us was to be "born again." This Greek expression can also be translated "born from above." Men and women can be made new — new creatures, the Bible says — by the power of heaven, the kingdom power of God.

Obviously people "born from above" would never be satisfied with a world which was only material. They need spiritual links as well as physical ones. The present world, with its limited scientific laws, is not big enough for a converted Christian anymore than a cage is for an eagle. It needs extending, and that extension goes beyond our three-dimensional world into the fourth dimension of the Spirit. We "walk in the Spirit" (Gal. 5:16). We are "seated with [Christ] in the heavenly realms" (Eph. 2:6, NIV).

The book of Acts shows the disciples drawing upon new resources as they moved through the world blessing the people with salvation and healing. The first new people in Christ, these new creatures of the kingdom, were sent out to bring others into the same kingdom order with new instincts, new powers and new laws written on their hearts (see Heb. 8).

After I was baptized in the Spirit and spoke with tongues, it didn't take me long to realize that this gift opened up new possibilities. If I spoke with tongues through the Spirit, then there could be other wonders through the Spirit. I have learned to live in the Spirit. I am on new ground where signs and wonders happen. Praise God!

If it weren't for that, nothing could happen as it does. Vast multitudes come to my meetings. They represent an intimidating accumulation of needs. But I am baptized in the Holy Spirit. I know the powers of the coming age and how to tap those resources. A great conviction grips me that God has something for them. That is not only my secret, but it is also the conviction of hundreds of millions today. If I have any other "secret" it is the message itself. I am confident of its effectiveness. It is "the power of God to salvation" (Rom. 1:16).

A Gospel That Isn't

If what we have been teaching so far is not what some readers have come to believe, we have to say that the gospel is being reinterpreted today in ways that take the heart out of it — and out of us. Liberal and rationalistic thought is based on the shifting sands of biblical criticism, speculation and philosophy. No assured grounds for the frightened millions have ever been offered by this new thought. It is a theology of chaff, a diet of starvation for those hungry for God. Too many scholars have made truth depend on

19

questions that can never have any certain answers, never reach finality — guesswork that is doomed to do absolutely nothing for lost nations and devil-stricken masses. If God is the only Savior, He cannot save by a message of "perhaps" or "if" or "it is my opinion." The world needs people with a live link to heaven.

For all classes of people, no matter how cultured or how primitive, there is one word of truth — the cross — to the wise, the barbarian, the Greek, the Jew, everyone. The gospel is the power of God. The gospel preacher is an ambassador demanding surrender to the kingdom of heaven. It is God's ultimatum. He shows us the way things are. The gospel is neither a theory nor an abstraction but the reality behind everything. We either recognize it or perish.

When you grasp what we are saying here, then you join the army with the battering ram of the Word and of the cross. It will pulverize the strongholds of the devil. It is the thundering drum-roll of God's invincible army on the march. When God filled me with His Spirit and opened my lips to speak with tongues, He opened my ears to hear the triumphant blast of the trumpet announcing that Jesus has all power in heaven and on earth. What a gift!

A God Identified by Miracles

Let me illustrate what I have said so far with actual examples. This chapter was begun in 1992 when I was in Brazzaville, the capital of the West African country of Congo. During a service, God gave me a word of knowledge for a couple otherwise unknown to me, somewhere among the tens of thousands present. A woman had been in a coma for three days and had been carried into the meeting by her husband. By faith and obedience to God's prompting I told the vast audience what the Spirit of the Lord had made known to me. As I spoke, the unconscious woman — though not hearing — came out of her coma and was healed. Mind over matter? Impossible — the patient knew nothing of what was going on till she revived.

Another lady present needed urgent surgery. Her unborn baby had died in her womb, and the hospital had arranged for the baby to be removed the next day. When prayer was offered for the mass of needy ones in the service, the baby in her womb leaped. She rushed forward to the platform tearfully to testify just in time, because straight afterward she went into labor. After being taken away, she gave birth to a bouncing baby boy.

These were not the only wonders that happened. They left me unable to sleep for excitement and joy. Most important of all, for six days the Holy Spirit swept through the crowd like a heavenly dam-burst, carrying one hundred thousand precious Congolese on a wave of blessing into the kingdom of God.

The Cross and Kingdom Miracles

The last of the basics to cover is this I have to show you that the power of the kingdom; the Holy Spirit and the gospel of the cross are welded together so that they cannot be separated. It was the work of Christ, especially in His death, which tore down the wall between this world and the other world of the kingdom of God. Since then the Holy Spirit has invested everything in the crucified Christ. He works His wonders solely on redemption ground. The Spirit supports the gospel only, always and everywhere.

What more do we need? One man filled with the Spirit is better than a hundred committees which "keep minutes but lose hours." When God so loved the world He didn't form a committee; He sent His Son, and His Son sent the Spirit. Christ said believers are the light of the world, but they need the Holy Spirit to switch them on.

No doubt many people reading this book are eager for miracles. There is nothing wrong with that. I want to help, and it will save many from disillusionment if I inform them that miracles belong only to the gospel — nothing else. No marvels for the sake of marvels. God isn't a showman. He is not in the business of supplying marvels to bring fame to any strutting egotist. The Holy Spirit is in league with the crucified Christ — even linked in name, the Spirit of Christ. They have one goal — to defeat the devil through the gospel.

The Spirit finds fulfillment only in the gospel. The gospel is so great. It is totally comprehensive, leaving nothing untouched — visible or invisible, earth, hell or heaven. Theologian George Lindberg in his book *The Nature of Doctrine* says, "A scriptural world is able to absorb the universe."

As a Christian I knew that the cross had a spiritual effect in my life, but when I spoke with tongues it reached me as an earthly person. The Father in heaven and the Son on earth are both concerned with redemption, each in His own sphere, as Jesus expressed in His prayer in John 17:4-5: "I have brought you glory on earth by completing the work you gave me to do. And now, Father, glorify me in your presence with the glory I had with you before the world began" (NIV).

These verses tell us that Christ's work on earth affected earth, and the Father's work affected glory. Jesus came here — for here. Hallelujah! If it was only to get us an entrance into heaven, He might have arranged it in heaven; but salvation had to be produced on earth for earthly purposes. My baptism in the Spirit touched both my spirit and my body, typical of the true nature of the Christian faith.

This truth makes all true Christian doctrine shine brighter. Salvation is not for part of a man but for the whole man. It is seen, for example, in healing, which is a spiritual and physical operation.

The Old Testament stresses the link between sickness and sin and the link between healing and forgiveness. That truth is refined in the New Testament. We shall come to that when we consider the gifts of healings.

2

God Has Taken the Field

In the first chapter we saw that the Christian age is also a new power age. A famous historian's words are interesting. Arnold Toynbee in his *Study of History* talks about "a new creative power flowing back into the historical process."[1] This is the kind of creative power that Jesus brought into the world. It is the Holy Spirit. The present expansion of churches which allow the Holy Spirit free expression is "the greatest religious phenomenon of our age," as *Time* magazine stated in 1971 — and that was only at the beginning of the greatest thrust.

Living in this world has been different since Jesus came. There is a new resource. The world of physical laws has been impacted by the spiritual laws of the world to come. The results are with us.

The Gospels introduce it, and the book of Acts gives the first reports of men and women as they accepted it. Now we shall look at some other aspects of this great change.

The Holy Spirit Kingdom Power

The Father gave us two gifts, both personal and equal. First He gave us His Son and then His Spirit. Jesus ranked the Spirit alongside Himself, describing Him as "another Comforter." He said it was better for the Spirit to come than for He Himself to remain with us in the flesh. The Holy Spirit's commission is to continue Christ's work of ministry on earth. Jesus healed the sick, for example, and the Holy Spirit follows the pattern of Christ.

How do we know who the Spirit is? The Holy Spirit is God in action. Whenever there are supernatural operations they are by the Spirit. All divine manifestations, such as the gifts, are always by the Spirit. When God moved on the world in the beginning it was by His Spirit. "The Spirit of God was hovering over the waters" (Gen. 1:2, NIV). The Father's will is spoken by the Word and performed by the Spirit. He executes the will of the Godhead.

The only Spirit Jesus promised us is the miracle Spirit, the Holy Spirit. There is no nonmiracle Holy Spirit. To claim to possess the Holy Spirit and deny the very work which has always distinguished Him can only grieve Him. It is He who began with the supreme physical wonder of creating the world. He doesn't change His nature. What He was, He is and always will be — God operating in the earthly sphere. "I am who I am" (Ex. 3:14). The Holy Spirit who made the world supernaturally should have no difficulty in continuing supernaturally.

John the Baptist, the divinely sent forerunner who introduced Christ, proclaimed a new era. "Repent, for the kingdom of heaven is at hand" (Matt. 3:2). The central core of that proclamation was the Messiah who would baptize in the Holy Spirit. It was far greater than the restoration of Israel's greatness — it was nothing less than a cosmic change. John unfolded a map of the future showing not a river of water but of fire. In Matthew 3:11, John used an earthly element, water, but Christ baptizes in a heavenly element, divine fire.

Jesus echoes the same words: "John baptized with water, but in a few days you will be baptized with the Holy Spirit" (Acts 1:5, NIV). We should take note of the fact that Jesus did not baptize anybody with the Spirit while He was on earth. John preached to people from "all the land of Judea, and those from Jerusalem...and [they] were all baptized by him in the Jordan River, confessing their sins" (Mark 1:5). It was to this random mass of people that John preached and declared, "I indeed baptized you with water, but He will baptize you with the Holy Spirit" (Mark 1:8). John laid down no special qualifications except repentance.

Many Baptisms

Before continuing we must look at the theory that the whole church was baptized in the Spirit forever on the day of Pentecost. Individuals can seek to be filled for themselves; however, but one filling of the Spirit is not lasting or enough, and we need to keep coming for a repeat experience — "many fillings."

But if the whole church was baptized forever on the day of Pentecost, why are Christians supposed to seek many fillings? We might ask if anyone listening to John or Christ ever dreamed they meant such a thing. We can't direct you to a Scripture that argues for this point, because there is not a single word about "repeated fillings." Neither is there the slightest suggestion that there would be a distinct baptism exclusively for an elite band of early disciples by proxy for the church of all time. Whether the Spirit comes at new birth or not, the first believers enjoyed a personal experience of the indwelling Spirit, and nothing less than that is offered to all who have believed since the day of Pentecost.

John plainly announced the purpose of Christ — to baptize men and women in the Spirit (Luke 3:16). It would characterize Him, giving Him the name of baptizer, just as John was the Baptist. Nobody can pretend that a single performance shows what we are. I once baked a cake, but it isn't typical of me; I would need a lot of urging to attempt it again. They don't call me a baker because of my sole success. I would have to bake cakes daily to bear the name of baker. Christ is called the Baptizer because that is His constant work, His heavenly office — the baptizer in the Holy Spirit, "the same yesterday, today, and forever" (Heb. 13:8).

Ronald W. Foulkes, a scholar commissioned by the Australian Methodist Charismatic Fellowship of Tasmania, offers a more technical explanation:

> There is a cliche, "One baptism, many fillings," but we should realize this is not scriptural; the biblical pattern and provision is for constant fullness. One is to go on being filled. The word "filled" is in a verbal form known as "ingressive aorist," suggesting an entrance into a state of condition. It is clear that the Christian who is baptized does not enter into a transitory experience, but into an abiding condition of fullness. Luke elaborates on the effect when speaking of Peter; he describes him as one "filled with the Holy Spirit" (Acts 4:8), using the passive participle of the aorist tense, indicating a happening in process.[2]

You will no doubt hear people talk about "one baptism, many fillings." Remember that these are the code words of those who oppose the baptism in the Spirit with signs following. But if charismatics or Pentecostals talk like this, we must ask a simple question: When someone says he or she has been baptized in the Spirit, how long does it last? a week? an hour? six months? Does the Holy Spirit leak away like power from a car battery? Is the baptism with the Spirit only one drink which we need to be refreshed with again and again? Another question is: How do we know when the Spirit has gone and we need another renewal? How long can we say, "I am Spirit-filled"? What signs indicate when we are and when we are not?

Jesus said that when the Comforter has come, "He [will] abide with you forever" (John 14:16). This is where the blessing of speaking with tongues is seen. We can't speak unless the Holy Spirit gives us utterance; if He does, He is there. By that sign we can go out and conquer, for He is with us. The Spirit abides with us. Our feelings are not a reliable indicator of the Holy Spirit's power within us. We need a sign which does not depend on our feelings.

History helps us here. In the nineteenth century, before tongues were commonly heard, the problem was knowing when the Spirit had come. People relied on intense and highly sensational moments. They would pray a great deal, believing that power could be measured by the time spent in prayer, an idea quite foreign to the Bible. At the dawn of the twentieth century it was taught for the first time that the sign of tongues *(glossolalia)* was the assurance of the baptism in the Spirit. This immediately triggered the greatest movement of the Holy Spirit of all time. My own faith was energized by the initial sign of tongues which led me into this present ministry of evangelism.

We can learn even more from Jesus in another passage. He spoke to the woman at the well in Samaria (John 4) and referred to "whoever drinks" (v. 14). The Greek tense He used (aorist) means to drink once only, not to keep coming back with an empty waterpot. That is the very thing the woman at the well of Sychar understood, for she said "that I...[need not] come here to draw" (v. 15). The one drink results in "a fountain of water springing up into everlasting life" (v. 14). Water is frequently used as a symbol of the Holy Spirit in Scripture, just as it is here.

"Another Comforter"

One thing has always amazed me. The disciples did not weep when Christ left them. They never showed any nostalgia for "the good old days." Luke tells us that after He ascended out of sight they "returned to Jerusalem with great joy, and were continually in the temple praising and blessing God" (Luke 24:52-53). Why did they display such a remarkable reaction to the departure of Jesus? The answer is the coming of the Spirit. When Christ was present they were only eyewitnesses of His power. But when the day of Pentecost came, they were more than eyewitnesses. They possessed power themselves and experienced the divine presence personally. It was different from when Christ was with them.

That personal sense of the presence of God is nowhere said to be just for the disciples alone, as if they were some kind of elite band. Peter said, "The promise is to you and to your children, and to all who are afar off, as many as the Lord our God will call" (Acts 2:39). He quoted the promise from Joel 2:28 in which God says, "I will pour out of My Spirit" (Acts 2:17). Wesley observes that this promise is not only for the day of Pentecost.[3] It describes the normal Christian experience, as does the whole book of Acts.

Another curious fact is that although Jesus told the disciples to take bread and wine in memory of Him, they never used the language of "remembering." One does not "remember" a person with whom he or she lives. He is a living and abiding presence by the

Spirit. "From now on, we regard no one according to the flesh. Even though we have known Christ according to the flesh, yet now we know Him thus no longer" (2 Cor. 5:16). To be filled with the Spirit brings us alive to Jesus, which is even better than being alive when Jesus was on earth.

Note too, that the Spirit does not come to talk about Himself but to reveal Jesus (John 16:15). Paul said he preached Christ crucified in the power and demonstration of the Spirit. If we only preach the power of the Spirit without the cross, we short-circuit the very power we preach about. The Spirit's primary interest is in the cross. We don't preach power, but the gospel of the cross which is the power of God by the Spirit.

Spirit-Galvanized

Speaking to the Fifth World Pentecostal Conference in 1953, Donald Gee said the Spirit was not "the subject of theological dogma, but a burning experience." He points out that when Paul dealt with problems in Galatia he appealed to their experience (Gal. 3:2). The Holy Spirit was God in earthly activity, just as Jesus had been.

The baptism in the Spirit is not meant to be a single emotional event recorded in believers' diaries. It envelops believers permanently. The Spirit is their environment, the air they breathe moment by moment which provides the vitality of their Christian faith. When we bombard the world with the artillery of the gospel, our ammunition is the explosive power of the Holy Spirit. The Spirit animates believers, their teachings, their preaching, their prayer, their service and their very lives.

The Spirit is the dynamic life force of the faith. Without the life of the Holy Spirit, Christianity is just another lifeless religious system that can only be kept going by human effort. But nothing can compete with the Holy Spirit. We can't replace the Holy Spirit with organization, magnificent churches, prestige, education or anything else.

When We Know, We Should Act

We have now gone a little way in our studies. Let me pause a moment to remind you that God Himself teaches us when we obey Him. If we learn these things, then we must understand that the Holy Spirit, God in action, leads *us* into action. We are not saved just to linger in fond contentment in the joy of salvation or to hold meetings to congratulate one another on our good fortune that we are redeemed.

There are higher activities than church celebrations, Christian pop music concerts and a seemingly endless flow of new worship songs — Christian as they may be. Our Lord is worthy to be praised indeed, but worship choruses alone will never save the world. Songs that do not mention the name of Jesus or have any gospel content are especially powerless. Praise is not the power of God unto salvation; the gospel is. We must not flatter ourselves into thinking that we can build a throne for God with lots of new songbooks. Our contract with God contains the clause "Preach the Word." "It pleased God by the foolishness of preaching to save them that believe" (1 Cor. 1:21, KJV).

We should do more than celebrate; we must communicate. As noted scholar Richard John Neuhaus once observed, "It is not our securities and satisfactions we celebrate, but the perilous business of love, of that supreme love that did not and does not turn back from the cross."

Some have said that there is more about fellowship than evangelism in the New Testament. This is a superficial point; there is no fellowship without evangelism. The word *fellowship (koinonia)* is much more than meeting our Christian friends in cozy comfort. It is sharing. We share the gospel and the fullness of the Spirit so that others have what we have. *Koinonia* depends on evangelism.

Rivers

Returning again to what Scripture says about the Holy Spirit, the word *rivers* is used repeatedly. It describes the ideal for believers, and "rivers" are the Holy Spirit. It was anticipated in Isaiah 58:11: "You shall be…like a spring of water, whose waters do not fail." A "rivers" experience requires the miracle presence of the Holy Spirit. For many people in our reserved Western culture, exuberance is foreign, unnatural and embarrassing. For those who stand within the kingdom of God, however, the culture of the world matters little. In our kingdom people shout for joy!

The Septuagint, the Greek version of the Old Testament, uses a surprising word about the Spirit of God acting in the lives of Samson and Saul. It says the Spirit "leapt" upon them. This rare word *(allomai)* is used twice in Acts 3:8 in the healing of the lame man — "leaping up" *(exallomenos)* and "leaping" *(allomenos)*. "Leaping life" and "dancing waters" are biblical descriptions of the activity of the Holy Spirit.

The Hebrew word for "worship," *kara*, signifies bodily action. Those blessed by the mighty Spirit of God, who leap for joy, are bound to appear strange. It is not surprising when people who have not been in the upper room of Pentecost deride Spirit-filled people as "enthusiasts" or "fanatics." Even the apostles had critics. The onlookers in Jerusalem thought the apostles were drunk. They were completely ignorant of the facts of the case.

That is why we should never be worried by critics. No doctrine, teaching or great work of God has ever remained unchallenged by those who thought they knew better. The Roman

Catholic writer and theologian Ronald A. Knox, for example, showed contempt for John Wesley by describing him as a mere "enthusiast" — an overwrought or unbalanced person. Father Knox may be an example of cool scholarship, but from his book *Enthusiasm* it is clear that he is not a man who would have been with the 120 on the day of Pentecost or stood shoeless at the burning bush with Moses or been with Joshua before the Man with the drawn sword. The intellectual bishop of Bristol, Joseph Butler, told Wesley that he considered charismatic experiences to be quite "horrid."[4]

O.T. Dobbin came to Wesley's defense in 1848: "We admit that Wesley was an enthusiast, but only to the degree in which a man more than ordinarily filled with the Holy Ghost would be an enthusiast."[5] Wesley's first rule for stewards of the Methodist Society, quoting Ephesians 3:16, was, "You are to be men full of the Holy Ghost."

George Whitefield, the great evangelist and fellow member of the Wesley brothers' Holy Club, was a man full of the Holy Spirit. During an evangelistic meeting at Fetter Lane in London, England on January 1, 1739, at three o'clock in the morning, the power of God prostrated many, and all cried out with joy, awe and amazement.

The question we must ask is this: If Christ did exactly what He promised and baptized people in the Holy Spirit and fire, what would they be like? Cool, English, self-contained? With glorious currents of divine radiance flowing through them, would they sit, as Shakespeare said, like their "grandsire cut in alabaster"?[6] The emblem of God is fire, not stone.

What is more ridiculous — people dancing for joy with the vision of God or people as immovable as the Sphinx (which remained unmoved even when Napoleon fired a cannon at it)? Flesh and blood are not like granite. We cannot experience the

Spirit and show no sign of it. What we have in earthen vessels is "treasure" which reveals that this all-surpassing power is from God (2 Cor. 4:7). This power will seem totally strange to minds alienated from God. As Festus said to Paul, "You are beside yourself! Much learning is driving you mad!" (Acts 26:24). Why should it be any different today when people experience the original brand of Christianity instead of some diluted, gutted, tranquilized, sentimentalized version of it? "You hath he quickened," we read in Ephesians 2:1 (KJV), not "You hath he stiffened."

Let's return to what we said earlier about the Holy Spirit as "rivers." In John 7:37-38, Jesus cried, "If any man thirst, let him come unto me, and drink. He that believeth on me as the Scripture hath said "out of his belly shall flow rivers of living water." This is quoted from the King James Version, but not exactly. I left out a comma, which makes a difference. No comma is there in the Greek original. So we should read it like this: "He that believeth on me as the Scripture hath said." That is, rivers of living water will flow from those who "believe on me as the Scripture has said." It is not living waters that Jesus says the Scripture talks about, but Himself and those who believe on Him. People have not found which Scripture Jesus had in mind when He spoke of waters, though we have suggested one above — Isaiah 58:11. The promise of living water originates with Jesus Himself, and as Peter preached, "The promise is to you and to your children, and to all who are afar off, as many as the Lord our God will call" (Acts 2:39).

It is even more important to look at John 3:34 again. The King James Version reads, "He whom God hath sent speaketh the words of God: for God giveth not the Spirit by measure *unto him.*" Now the words shown in italics, "unto him," are not in the original text. The NIV translates it correctly: "God gives the Spirit without limit" — that is, to us all, as John 1:16 tells us, "Of His fullness we have all received." Literally "because of his fullness" we are filled without measure.

Fullness lies in Christ Jesus and flows out of Him to fill us. He is the source. So long as Christ is full, we shall "be being filled." He is "full of grace and truth" (John 1:14), and out of Him we receive "grace for grace" (v. 16), or grace constantly being renewed.

As Christians, we are not set up in business all on our own with a lump sum of spiritual capital and power resources to make us independent. We are not self-sufficient little Christs or replicas of the Son of God who alone had immortality. Those who teach such a thing reveal gross theological ignorance. As the branches of a vine receive sap, so we receive moment by moment from Christ "out of" His fullness, "the fullness of him who fills everything in every way" (Eph. 1:23, NIV). We are not vines ourselves living separate existences.

The Spirit's Difference

The prophets struggled in vain to bring Israel back to God. But when Peter, who was full of the Spirit, preached, three thousand people surrendered to God. Without the Holy Spirit, Christianity is reduced to religion which is no more effective than the Old Testament system and the priesthood which existed before the age of the Spirit.

Jesus said, "You will receive power when the Holy Spirit comes on you" (Acts 1:8, NIV). Without that vitality we have a secularized, nominalized, anglicized, rationalized and harmless religion. Mystical contemplation bears no resemblance to New Testament dynamism. Quietism is for Buddhists, not Christians.

Before the charismatics arrived, there were those who were fired up and Spirit-filled, or "pneumatized." Whatever chill may have frozen the church, however much "enthusiasm" was disapproved of, and even when Christianity was only "churchianity," there were always some lively Spirit-filled people around. The springs of spiritual waters in this century came from rains which fell centuries before. Some trace them to Wesley and his teaching which he called "perfect love." But whatever it was called, the vision and experience Wesley had came from earlier men and women of God.

Call It What You Like

Many different terms are used for the same experiences in Scripture. All the terms, such as "coming upon," "being filled," "drinking" and "anointing," describe the same divine gift of the Spirit. Christ said we should "ask...seek...knock" (Matt. 7:7). This applies to receiving the baptism of the Spirit also. Those who receive the Spirit in New Testament style surely have a right to call their experience by a New Testament name.

The "baptism in the Holy Spirit" is a New Testament expression used by both John the Baptist and Jesus. The personal experience of millions conforms to the New Testament promise whether it is called baptism or anything else. If it looks like such a baptism, sounds like it, feels like it and operates like it, then what else is it? It cannot be argued out of existence by debates about what to call it. If we do what the apostles did and we get what the apostles got, its name doesn't matter.

But there has been opposition, and there still is. It does seem suspicious, though, that nobody invented any teaching against an after-conversion receiving of the Spirit until the "tongues people" began to be noticed. History shows that the church has always assumed that receiving the Holy Spirit was a separate experience. From the earliest times when people were baptized they were anointed afterward to receive the Spirit. It was called "chrism." [7]

Various liturgies showed that "chrism," the anointing with oil, was given only to those baptized and said to be children of God and in the kingdom. A candidate was considered unfit to receive the Spirit until regenerated. In the Anglican church confirmation after baptism has been taken as the moment when the Spirit is imparted by the laying on of hands by the bishop.

Let us look at this a little further. If everyone received the Spirit by proxy on the day of Pentecost, as some teach, why do they pray for the "many fillings"? What use was the baptism on the day of Pentecost if each person needs filling again and again? What seems to be overlooked is that all these fillings are after-conversion experiences.

That is one thing we should not overlook. Some receive a mighty baptism at the same time as conversion, as did Cornelius and his household in Acts 10, but not everyone did or does. But whether one receives it at new birth or some later time does not alter the fact that this great experience actually exists. For the disciples and millions of others, it came later.

If the enduement with the Holy Spirit and power always comes with new birth, we wonder why those who believe it still seek God for power. If the baptism of the Spirit takes place at conversion for everybody, why isn't it more obvious? The mark of the great revivalists and the sweeping power of the present spiritual outpouring has been some kind of further experience or experiences in which God came in an extraordinary way.

The Effect of the Spirit

We now go on to see what the effects of being filled with the Spirit should be.

Being filled with the Spirit is shown to have a dynamic and energizing effect or "power" *(dunamis)* in the New Testament and in the lives of millions. There is little Scripture to suggest that the Spirit comes upon men like a quiet breath, unobtrusive and unnoticed. It is usually very noticeable — manifestations of the Spirit include fire, wind, noise, wonders, outward signs, powers and visible effects. God does not give His gifts to the unconverted nor His Holy Spirit to the world, but when we are born again we are encouraged to be filled, just as Paul admonished the churches (Eph. 5:18).

I must emphasize again that we are seeing what Scripture says about these things. Some turn to church history. They try to prove that apostolic power died out with the apostles. Church history, not the Bible, settles their doctrine. They could profitably have wondered why it died down at the end of the apostolic age (though in fact it did not completely vanish). But there is not a single scrap of Bible evidence to indicate that it should have done this. A true scholar would want to know why. If we have learned anything from church history we know that unbelief and spiritual decline set in, and the power of the Spirit was therefore unlikely to be manifested widely.

Christianity was never intended to be anything but an outpouring of the Spirit. It is a reviving, quickening, renewing energy. Revival is not an extraordinary work above and beyond normal Christianity. Christianity *is* revival. There are not two Spirits, the Spirit received at new birth and the Spirit of revival which sometimes comes down from heaven and takes the field. The Spirit of God took the field long ago and has never withdrawn from the battle. He does not visit it now and then. He came to stay permanently. Having put His hand to the plow He did not look back. Revival is always there when the Word is preached and the Spirit is present.

Both David and Isaiah prayed, "Lord, rend the heavens and come down" (see Ps. 144:5; Is. 64:1). It happened when Jesus came. New Testament believers need never pray it again. Christ tore the heavens and came down to us. He then returned through the heavens ensuring that they remain open. The rent heavens have been opened forever and have never been sewn up again, either by a needle-wielding Satan or any other hand. Through that open heaven the Holy Spirit then began to descend — the latter rain. Hell cannot impose sanctions and blockade the kingdom of God, nor deprive its citizens. The new and living way is established beyond enemy control.

In his book *Joy Unspeakable*, the great teacher D. Martyn Lloyd-Jones concluded that revival is the baptism in the Holy Spirit.[8] He lays down firm proof that there is a scriptural reception of power after conversion, that it is the baptism with the Spirit, and that it is revival. Since 1901 when that truth was recovered, the restoration of Bible signs and wonders has brought hundreds of millions into the kingdom of God.

No New Testament Christian confined himself to religious meditation. Mystics usually end up with erroneous teachings. The apostles were activists. Smith Wigglesworth was right: "The Acts of the Apostles was written because the apostles acted." They did not visit shrines or keep the relics of holy men. They were in vital contact with God themselves through the Spirit. They went directly to Him, not through saints and their bones.

The entire Christian life is "in the Spirit." By the Spirit the Son of God was the Anointed One. This set the pattern. Just as He went about doing good because He was anointed with the Spirit, so must we. Like Jesus we are told to walk in the Spirit, pray in the Spirit, love in the Spirit, live in the Spirit, be filled with the Spirit, sing in the Spirit and have the fruit of the Spirit.

The Spirit-filled life is not an experience to be cultivated in special conditions, like indoor crocuses. Christians are not flowers, and they don't believe in flower power. During the early expansion of the industrial cities of England some clergymen could not be persuaded to take a parish among the hordes of unwashed workers because they said it might spoil their "spirituality." The Holy Spirit makes believers tough specimens for all conditions. They carry perpetual springtime in their souls and are "winterized" just as homes are prepared for the cold weather.

The apostles discovered a new resilience, a new strength within them, a power that operated in their weakness and sent them out into a brutal pagan world to demolish its idol establishment and change history. That is a true mark of the Spirit-filled life.

Things like that are happening today. A new age of persecution is testing the church throughout the world. We may have to lay down our physical lives, but we are proving that the baptism in the Spirit makes people undefeatable.

3

THE ANOINTING

oly Spirit anointing is fully scriptural. I know that new experiences for believers which have never been heard of before are being discovered and promoted, such as "the breakthrough" or perpetual penitence. Anointing is sometimes taken as one of the latest "in" things for those seeking a higher stratum of spirituality, but it is not new. In the Old Testament all who served God had to be anointed. This is replaced in the New Testament by the Holy Spirit for all believers.

First, *anointing* is one of the synonyms of the baptism in the Spirit; there are others.

For years we have sung with Psalm 23, "My head thou dost with oil anoint." One commentary suggests that there was actually a practice in Old Testament days of oiling the head of sheep for their protection, but the anointing of the Spirit, or the baptism with the Spirit, is much more than a protective measure.[1] It refers to the anointing of the Spirit, or the baptism with the Spirit.

Let us see what we can learn in the house of Simon the Pharisee. Jesus is making a complaint using similar language to that in Psalm 23. He is saying to his host, "My head with oil thou didst not anoint" (Luke 7:46, KJV). He was comparing Simon and an unknown woman. She had poured perfumed oil upon His feet and continued kissing His feet, but Simon had done nothing. It was the social welcome for guests to anoint them with fragrant oils and greet them with the double kiss on the cheeks — as is still the practice in the East. Simon had been too casual and showed Jesus no such respect.

The social anointing of guests was meant to impart a pleasant smell to the guests and to help their appearance by making their faces shine (Ps. 104:15). An oiled and shining face was considered admirable in those days. Cones of perfumed ointment were placed on the heads of guests so that when they became warm it would trickle down their faces onto their clothes and pervade the atmosphere with a pleasant odor. Jesus accepted the anointing from this woman who lavished Him with the best ointment that money could buy.

Mary also anointed Jesus. Her ointment was spikenard, a very rare and precious preparation of nard brought from northern India at great expense and prepared with the secretive art of the perfumer. Sold in long, slender alabaster containers, it kept for years and would even improve in quality and value. Many of these containers have been found on archaeological sites. When filled with ointment they were kept as an investment, a household treasure.

The fragrance of Mary's oil was so rich we are told it pervaded the whole house. It was a tremendous sacrifice, an act of love's bountiful extravagance. It speaks of the love of God through Jesus Christ which brings us the priceless gift of the anointing of the Holy Spirit. It is no cheap experience. It is God's best.

The most common ingredient of cosmetic ointment was myrrh, which was refined from a perfumed, resinous substance produced most commonly from the small *commiphora myrrha nees* tree. We often read of it in Scripture. The girl loved by Solomon had fingers which dripped with sweet-smelling myrrh. Solomon himself came from the dusty wilderness "perfumed with myrrh and frankincense" (Song 3:6). Part of the beauty treatment for Esther's presentation to King Xerxes was six months with oil of myrrh (see Esth. 2:12).

The value of it is shown when the Magi brought myrrh to the baby Jesus as a special gift. People carried myrrh in their clothes. Taken medically, myrrh was used as an opiate. Jesus refused it on the cross.

The use of anointing oil originated in the pouring of ointment upon priests to ordain them for service. Theirs was a special anointing oil described in Exodus 30 and used only for the Lord's tabernacle and priests. Kings were also anointed. Most commentaries also say prophets were anointed, but from what I can see in Scripture not one of them ever was. They were never appointed to be a prophet as if it were to an office, like priest or king. They were independent men of God, not socially appointed. God chose and gave them the real anointing with the Spirit. Nobody made prophets. They were God's men. By divine command Elijah should have anointed Elisha but failed to do so. God Himself anointed Elisha with the Spirit.

It was the habit to call the Spirit of God by the name of a prophet — the spirit of Moses or the spirit of Elijah — as a personal and rare distinction. The spirit of Moses was to be put upon the elders of Israel, and Elisha wanted a double portion of the spirit of Elijah. The Spirit was identified with the prophet, and when God anoints believers today it is with "the spirit of the prophets" or the "spirit of prophecy."

The true anointing is always by the Lord. Oils, unguents and ointments were poured upon priests and kings as mere symbols or acknowledgments that God's Spirit had chosen to rest upon them. God was the originator, and such men were therefore called "the anointed of the Lord" and "the anointed of God" — especially Christ (from "Messiah" or "anointed"), who is "the anointed of God" (see Matt. 1:17). Today among believers the anointing is a sovereign act of God.

Disciples and apostles were never anointed with oil. In the New Testament Christians received the Spirit for their work of service. Oil was never poured upon Jesus, except by a woman for His burial, as He said. Before the day of Pentecost priests were anointed and carried the fragrance with them, but since the day of Pentecost believers have carried the aura of Jesus. "They realized that they had been with Jesus" (Acts 4:13). The real anointing had come.

Anointing with oil was retained only for the healing of the sick in the New Testament (see James 5:14).

Our anointing flows out of Christ's anointing, and we receive it only from Him. "Of His fullness we have all received" (John 1:16). To John the Baptist it was revealed that "the man on whom you see the Spirit come down and remain is he who will baptize with the Holy Spirit" (John 1:33, NIV). He — nobody else. He identified the source, Jesus Christ, the giver and the authority of the giving.

We may pray and lay hands on people to be baptized in the Spirit, as the apostles did (Acts 8:17), but we must realize that a man cannot and need not give his anointing to someone else. It is out of Christ's fullness, not somebody else's fullness. I want my own anointing from God, not a secondhand anointing. To bestow an anointing, even as a temporary effect, is foreign to Bible thought.

It comes "out of His fullness" as a constant outflow. He alone is the baptizer. The blessings of God may flow in many ways through our lives as rivers of living water from Christ, but that is very different from doing what only Jesus can do — impart the Spirit. The virgins refused to share their oil and were counted wise (Matt. 25:7-10).

However, the word *anointing* today has acquired a broader meaning among believers. It is a word for general blessing. When people offer to bring us "an anointing" by laying their hands upon us we need not object. Scripturally there is no such thing as an anointing, only the anointing. But we need not be pedantic about the use of a word, providing, of course, that it does not convey bad theology or that the exclusive sense of giving the Holy Spirit is not intended but only a prayer for help, strength or any other need.

Once, by divine leading, I found myself far from where I should have been, staring at a house in Clapham, London. A board outside referred to George Jeffreys, whom many consider to have been the greatest British revivalist since John Wesley. He filled the greatest halls, pioneered in the face of universal opposition and proclaimed the glorious message of Jesus Christ, Savior, healer, baptizer and coming king. I could hardly believe it — I had just read one of this great man's books. Was he really there?

I dared to go and ask; he heard my voice and invited me in. There he prayed with me, and it was as if his mantle had come upon me (to use a scriptural expression). God heard that man's prayer for me. I was already baptized in the Spirit — anointed — but sometimes we lack language to describe all that God does. I know that making contact with George Jeffreys and hearing his prayer for me had been a special experience which brought me a sense of equipping and readiness for service. Earlier that day I had left the Bible college at Swansea to begin my full-time service for God. God had called me to His work, and now this special experience seemed to cover me.

David was anointed by Samuel as king, which David took to mean that he was the Lord's anointed. Later the elders of Israel also anointed him as their assurance of his call to them as king. Anointings are not to be expected every time we meet a special evangelist or teacher. For me it was only once, after my call, when I met a man who had done the same work as God wanted me to do. It was like Elisha following Elijah.

Some experiences, which we may call anointings (for lack of a better expression), may come as the assurance of God to a particular call, like that of the elders of Israel, David and Elisha. To some they have come when listening to some other man of God, when they knew God was thrusting them forward as what Paul calls "the more honorable" members of the body of Christ (1 Cor. 12:23-24).

George Canty, my co-writer, had been put off by the methods of some healing evangelists and was critical of such activity. God had been pressuring him for some time, asking him, "Where are all your mighty miracles?" One day he sat listening as a healing evangelist spoke. As soon as the man quoted his text, George Canty felt a sudden spiritual elevation to a new plane. He knew he would do what the preacher had done and heal sick people. The impression was so vivid he had to look around to assure himself that the building was real, because it seemed such a visionary and transcendent moment. He knew he was different from that moment on.

Anointing and appointing go together. The only people anointed were those selected for a particular task, especially that of priest or king. It was not an experience for mere emotional enjoyment.

Anointing did not signify that a special level of holiness had been attained. The anointing was given solely to equip and condition ordinary people to serve the Lord. The anointing was not available apart from service. Today, the anointing is for all believers, for all are to serve — we are "a royal priesthood" (1 Pet. 2:9).

Note carefully that anointing is not a kind of emotional pleasure, but it comes into activity when we serve. David did not feel anointed in any particular sense, but when he faced Goliath his anointing became apparent. Samson became strong only when he went into action for God. Then the Spirit of God came upon him (see Judg. 14:6). A strong man does not feel his strength when he's sitting down — only when he exerts himself.

The Anointed One

Now we will look at some other considerations. We should particularly remember that anointing was like a perfume. Psalm 45:6-7 is quoted in the New Testament (Heb. 1:8-9) as referring to Christ. It is interesting to note that verse 8 of that psalm goes on: "All Your garments are scented with myrrh and aloes and cassia." Cassia came from the distant Far East. Israel probably obtained it in the wilderness from passing traders. It provided a distinctive fragrance associated only with the dwelling place of God and its priests — it evoked thoughts of God.

Scripture calls Jesus *the* Anointed One. "Peter answered and said, You are the Christ [the Anointed One], the Son of the living God" (Matt. 16:16). He was the Christ. Jesus is as exclusively anointed as He was exclusively the Son of God. "Christ" is from the Greek *christos* which translates as the Hebrew "Messiah."

Everything denoted by the anointing of the tabernacle and priests and kings is fulfilled in Jesus. Christ is our priest-king. "Your garments are scented..." (Ps. 45:8). He carried the purity and odor of heaven, that evocative and subtle beauty of spirit which makes Him the Anointed One, distinguished from all others. He drew people, not merely by power or "charisma" in the popular sense, but by love, moving in the atmosphere of His own holiness which people had never breathed before. If we can put it this way, Jesus was God's alabaster box, broken for us on the cross and now filling the world with His fragrance.

Personal beauty is never condemned in Scripture. Pride, lack of modesty, provocative dress and brazen flirting certainly are. God makes people beautiful and does not expect us to belong to the cult of ugliness and make the worst of ourselve. I don't believe God took pleasure in the "saints" of the early centuries who boasted of the population of lice in their hair and beards. Nor was He pleased with the nuns who boasted that water never touched their feet except when they crossed a river. God does not give special honor to those who dress out-of-fashion, dowdy or drab to win His favor. He creates beautiful things, from the glory of the dawn and majesty of the sunset to the star-spangled velvet of the night sky. His dwelling is the light of the setting sun. Our very means and ability to create beauty come from Him. Scripture says He makes "everything beautiful in its time" (Eccl. 3:11). "Let the beauty of the Lord our God be upon us" (Ps. 90:17). That is what the anointing is.

"The beauty of holiness" forbids pride. Pride is the "dead flies" which "cause [the ointment] to give off a foul odor" (Eccl. 10:1). Our proud efforts at holiness are described in Isaiah 64:6: "All our righteous acts are like filthy rags" (NIV). That is because they produce a judgmental and condemnatory attitude toward those who we suppose have lower standards. We put on spiritual airs with an unattractive, narrow and negative correctness. A legalistic life has about as much chance of producing true fruit of the Spirit as arctic ice has of producing orchids.

Gifts or the Giver

It is absolutely necessary to learn next that the Holy Spirit is "He," not "it." The Spirit is not an impersonal force or mere spiritual electricity. The anointing of God is not just power or gifts, but the Holy Spirit Himself.

When people speaking with tongues first stepped into modern history, they were called "the tongues people" and similar names by many well-known British evangelicals such as Meyer, Morgan, Anderson, Scroggie and others who were opposed to the experience.[2] In fact, the memory of those people is still among us. They carried an impressive godliness motivated by service, not sensation, seeking the Giver, not the gifts. They wanted to know Jesus better and be Christ-like. They did not seek power for the sake of power. Their daily desire was to "let this mind be in [them] which was also in Christ Jesus, who...made Himself of no reputation, taking the form of a servant...and became obedient" (Phil. 2:5-8). Many laid down their lives for God.

When Jesus healed the sick it was not just sheer electric power He wielded but the power of His conquering love. He healed the sick by His stripes (Is. 53:5) — that was the secret wonder of His anointing. He healed a withered arm even though it provoked men to plot against His life. He risked everything and would go to any lengths, even the cross, for the sake of those who were suffering.

Pain and the ministry of healing are strangely linked. If we are willing to know "the fellowship of His sufferings" (Phil. 3:10), then we will feel the same anointing of love that Jesus had. If we have the same heartbreaking pity that forgets self and will make any sacrifice for the afflicted as Jesus did, then we will identify with those who suffer, sharing their suffering to ease their pain. If we are "touched with the feeling of [their] infirmities" (Heb. 4:15, KJV) as Jesus was, and realize for ourselves what 1 Corinthians 12:26

means when it says, "If one part suffers, every part suffers with it" (NIV), then perhaps fewer people would go home unhealed. I know nothing more profane than healing the sick in Jesus' name to get rich or to make a name for oneself or for the gratification of wielding power.

A New Anointing?

We have already established that God never anointed anybody twice. David was anointed of the Lord through Samuel, but later the elders of Israel did anoint him a second time, thus confirming their acceptance of his kingly authority and divine anointing. Jesus was anointed by God. Afterward women poured ointment on Him, which He said was for His burial, a very special part of His service to the Father and for mankind. Other than these examples, priests or kings only had an initial anointing at the beginning of their career.

Some sing for a new anointing and pray for another Pentecost. But the whole concept of "another" or "new" anointing — as if the original anointing had faded away — is strange to New Testament thought on the eternal Spirit. The anointing is self-renewing — it renews us, we don't renew it. He is the Spirit of newness. "He abides, Hallelujah, He abides with me!"[3] we sing, just as Jesus promised. First John 2:27 says, "The anointing which you have received from Him abides in you." In Exodus 40:15 we read, "You shall anoint them...that they may minister to Me." Second Samuel 1:21 speaks of the "shield of the mighty" being anointed for battle, and the eighth chapter of Leviticus tells us of the anointing for sanctified service and holiness.

We can lay our hands upon our friends and pray to bring God's strength and blessing, but we must not suppose we can fill a person with the Spirit each time, assuming the enduement has died away. The Holy Spirit does not evaporate! If we are doing the work to which God has called us, the anointing rests upon us without ever diminishing. It is in the same pattern as "eternal life" — we receive it moment by moment, like a waterfall fed by a never-failing river. All that is necessary is that we release His energies by working in His name.

The anointing is not to make us as conspicuous as Joseph in his coat of many colors. In a TV commercial a young lady with a very bad cold who has lost her sense of smell sprays herself with more and more perfume. When she opens the door to her admirer, her perfume overpowers him and knocks him down! It is human to want overwhelming power with an impact that everyone can feel. John the Baptist wore conspicuous rough clothing and ate peculiar food. This indicated that he was a holy prophet. Jesus did neither. He dressed inconspicuously and ate anything set before Him. Many were awed in the presence of Jesus, but it was not by demonstrations of overwhelming power. It came as concern and love for men and women. That is why they fell down and worshipped Him.

In ourselves, sinful and limited, we are completely unfit to become the temples of the Spirit, but we are. We wonder and worship. When that mighty Spirit takes up His abode within us, then oil, hands or anything else upon our outer flesh are only symbols of His indwelling greatness.

Along with anointing, as we said, there are other symbols of the Spirit. But we have carefully examined anointing for a very good reason. What we are trying to teach in this book cannot be as mere learned head knowledge, but it must enter the heart and be expressed in the life; it must "take root downward, and bear fruit upward" (Is. 37:31).

Paul wrote to the Philippians about the beauty of Christ's humility and went on to mention two women who were at odds,

Syntyche and Euodia. Then with great tact he thanked the Philippians for their recent kindness and described it as "a sweet-smelling aroma" — in Greek, *euodia*, a gentle hint to Euodia herself (Phil. 4:2).

The inward Spirit is seen by outward effects, physical indications of an inward and spiritual source. To desire power merely to show off is corrupting and odious, not fragrant. The real power of God only comes with the Holy Spirit, who reveals the loveliness of the Christ life and His graciousness — "Love to the loveless shown that they might lovely be."[4]

4

HOW THE GIFTS CAME

Now we turn our attention to the whole question of how the gifts of the Spirit became available to us today. A little word of caution first. Receiving the Holy Spirit and His gifts has been marred by many innovative and novel approaches. Some realignment to the Word of God is needed in this area. The gifts are not tricks, techniques or abilities we can pick up by watching others. God is pouring out His Spirit, and He does not need mere imitations of the gifts.

It is not a matter of learning the correct approach and striving to obtain the gifts as prizes to be won. Gifts are not only for spiritual athletes. If they were prizes to be won they would not be gifts. Gifts are for those in the kingdom of God — they belong there.

Israel's blessings are covenanted to the commonwealth of Israel. Christ Jesus linked wonders to the new Christian commonwealth: "If I cast out demons with the finger of God, surely the kingdom of God is come upon you" (Luke 11:20).

The "finger of God" is the Holy Spirit, as Peter tells us: "God anointed Jesus of Nazareth with the Holy Spirit and power, and...he went around...healing all who were under the power of the devil" (Acts 10:38, NIV). There is no power greater than that of the Holy Spirit. That is kingdom power, and no other power matches it. By the Spirit He distributes His ministries to whom He chooses.

Miracles Characterize the Kingdom

My assurance to all readers and learners is that miracles are normal for the kingdom. Christ sent His disciples out and said, "When you enter a town and are welcomed...heal the sick who are there and tell them, 'The kingdom of God is near you'" (Luke 10:8-9, NIV). Before Christ, in Old Testament times, miracles were rare, being special, historic visitations of God that were divinely brought about by His sovereign will.

There were no gifts of healings for the blind, crippled or deaf. Outstanding people such as David, Ezra, Nehemiah, Jeremiah and Esther never once witnessed a physical wonder, and some never experienced anything they could call supernatural. Ezra never felt the moving of the Spirit. He never had a vision, a call, a voice or even an appointment as a prophet. He could trust the Word alone. Generally the few signs and wonders that were seen were demonstrations to reprove rulers, such as the despotic lords of Egypt, Babylon and Israel. These wonders were aimed at humbling them, as they did with Nebuchadnezzar. He was forced to admit that God's "dominion is an eternal dominion; his kingdom endures from generation to generation...I...glorify the King of heaven" (Dan. 4:34, 37, NIV).

Usually such events were judgments, like the plagues of Egypt. But the higher qualities of kingdom power were kindness and mercy. John the Baptist, the last of the Old Testament prophets, expected harsh judgment when the Messiah came. He spoke of the fire cleansing and burning up the chaff. But when Jesus baptized with fire rather than destruction and judgment, the blaze of love came. Jesus healed the sick. Jesus sent John the Baptist a message to show that His fire was His rage against the evils men suffered. He was the One who should come. The gifts of the Spirit are benevolent and kind.

The same kind of contrast between John and Jesus is seen between Elijah and Elisha, one a prophet of fire and judgment and his successor a prophet of kingdom mercies.

When Jesus met a blind man He said, "I must work the works of Him who sent Me while it is day" (John 9:3). By this He showed that the restoration of the blind was His Father's work. Kingdom mercies continued as long as Jesus was in the world. Moreover, they eventually resumed after He had gone. Jesus said to His disciples, "The night is coming when no one can work" (John 9:4). He meant that soon He would be crucified, night would fall, and there would be no blind receiving their sight. He said to the disciples, "Without Me you can do nothing" (John 15:5). And they did not for a long time. Then they received what Jesus had promised — power when the Holy Spirit came.

Power by Baptism in the Spirit

Now if the power of the kingdom is the Holy Spirit, then kingdom power was given to the church on the day of Pentecost. This is more than power and authority. In a saying of key importance

Christ announced to His followers, "It is your Father's good pleasure to give you the kingdom" (Luke 12:32).

Believers inherit the kingdom "lock, stock and barrel." The kingdom power which rested on Christ Jesus was for working signs and wonders. The same Spirit is given to those within the kingdom of God for the same kingdom purposes. As John the Baptist revealed: "The man on whom you see the Spirit come down and remain is he who will baptize with the Holy Spirit" (John 1:33-34, NIV). The Spirit endowed Jesus and His people with the same power.

There is a difference between Christ and His followers — it is rather noticeable! The difference is first who He is. Those who say, "The words of Christ on our lips are the same as on Christ's lips," must remember this: It is not the words which matter, but the person who speaks them. We may be adopted sons of God, but He is the eternal and only begotten. The second difference is that the Spirit comes from Him. He is the source. We are not sources, but channels — riverbeds through which the waters of His fullness flow.

Before Christ, nobody had been baptized in the Spirit. This term means something different from the attachment of the Spirit to Old Testament men and women. First Samuel 16:13 says Samuel took the horn of oil and anointed David, and the Spirit of the Lord "came upon David from that day forward." But such experiences are never described as a baptism, for the Holy Spirit's relationship with blood-washed, born-again believers is new. John 14:17 says that the Spirit was *with* them but would be *in* them. That is why a new expression is used. It describes a new kind of experience. To deny Christians the right to use the phrase *baptized in the Spirit* leaves them limited to the same kind of experience as in the Old Testament dispensation.

Parakletos

The old covenant people knew nothing of speaking with tongues, casting out demons and healing by the laying on of hands. These signs were reserved for the age of the Spirit (Mark 16:17). A new kingdom, a new covenant with new features, a new gospel for spirit and body describe the Christian age. Jesus used a new word for the Holy Spirit — *parakletos* — used five times in John's Gospel. It is translated "Comforter" (KJV), "Counselor" (NIV). It belongs to the Greek word *parakaleo*, to call for somebody, to enlist their sympathy, and is translated comfort, consolation.

Think about the promise of "another comforter." To understand this, we need only emphasize the word *Comforter*. He Himself had been the *parakletos* to His disciples. Jesus said, "I will not leave you comfortless" (John 14:18, KJV). In this case the Greek word is *orphanous* (orphans), as in James 1:27, "fatherless" (KJV). Jesus constantly used only one word for God, "the Father," and that is the relationship He has established for all who receive Him, the Son of God. So when He gave His last assurances to His disciples in Acts 1:4-5, He said, "Wait for the gift my Father promised...you will be baptized with the Holy Spirit" (NIV). He also related the gift of the Spirit to the Father in Luke 11:13: "How much more will your heavenly Father give the Holy Spirit to those who ask Him!" If we were orphans, we would not receive the Spirit. "Those who are led by the Spirit of God are sons of God" (Rom. 8:14, NIV).

A breathtaking view of the kingdom is shown to us in John 14:12: "Anyone who has faith in me will do what I have been doing. He will do even greater things than these, because I am going to the Father" (NIV). The word for "greater," *meizona*, does not specify what order of greatness, whether in number, quality or magnitude. This has been a problem to many Bible students.

Surely nothing could outclass the miracles of Jesus in intrinsic omnipotence, such as the raising of Lazarus.

There are two senses in which someone can do greater things than Christ. Obviously there are some works of His we could never do since He is the Son of God. He is the only Redeemer. He alone could die for the sins of the whole world. The works He referred to were works of mercy, deliverance, healing and aid. First, there could be more numerous instances, and second, they could be spread over a wider area. Both took place as the disciples moved out in missionary travel.

For centuries, since the invention of printing and modern technology, far more vast operations can bring results impossible even for Jesus when He was localized in this or that village or town. He was physically limited, but not limited in power. He needed more hands, more voices — more extensions of Himself — for we are members of the body of Christ (Rom. 12:4-5; 1 Cor. 6:15; 12:12, 18, 27; Eph. 5:30). The hymn writer expresses it this way: "The arms of love that compass me would all mankind embrace."[1] They are our arms, but also His.

This could only be possible through the power of the Spirit. Jesus repeated this emphatically:

> I tell you the truth, anyone who has faith in me will do what I have been doing. He will do even greater things than these, because I am going to the Father...It is for your good [Greek *sympherei*; expedient, advantageous] that I am going away. Unless I go away, the Counselor will not come to you (John 14:12; 16:7, NIV).

This is our basis for the gifts of the Spirit.

The World Bursts Into View

Reading the Bible from the beginning we find ourselves being told about nothing but Israel — book after book, as if God were only the God of the Jews and had limited His interests to that tiny land and small nation. But as soon as we open the New Testament, the borders melt away, and the wide world comes into view. True, Jesus did say (of His own ministry), "I was sent only to the lost sheep of Israel" (Matt. 15:24, NIV). But on that same occasion he healed a girl who did not belong to Israel, but to Canaan. He spoke about that same area in Nazareth concerning the widow helped by Elijah (Luke 4:25-27; 1 Kin. 17:8-24). His statement against racial discrimination infuriated the congregation, but He went to Canaan later.

After Christ rose from the dead, the disciples retained a Jewish outlook for a long time and saw their new faith as belonging to Israel only. They even asked the Lord an hour or so before He ascended, "Are you at this time going to restore the kingdom to Israel?" Jesus replied, "It is not for you to know...but you will receive power when the Holy Spirit comes on you; and you will be my witnesses...to the ends of the earth" (Acts 1:6-8, NIV). When the Holy Spirit fell, they spoke with the tongues of people from many different countries, displaying the ethnic interests of the Holy Spirit. What God did at Babel, scattering the people by confounding their languages, He reversed at Pentecost, uniting them by different languages.

Kingdom Secret

The gospel the disciples preached as they went out was the gospel of the kingdom of God — the good news that the kingdom was close to them. But they preached it in new terms not used by

John the Baptist and only occasionally used by Jesus Himself. Their kingdom gospel was proclaimed in the language of Christ crucified. It was not a different gospel, but it contained a tremendous new fact — the vital fact about the kingdom — the cross. When Jesus had spoken of it earlier, Peter had even tried to rebuke Christ (Matt. 16:22). What at first seemed outrageous to the disciples was, they later realized, the all-important mystery of the kingdom, the self-sacrifice of the king for the kingdom.

The kingdom is established by the titanic battle and victory of Christ. His blood marks its foundations. Calvary is the source of the redemptive dynamic of God, the nuclear power drive of the gospel and of all the gifts of the Spirit.

For those moving into a real charismatic relationship, we are obliged to mention that modern religionists are busy building Calvary bypasses. The gospel of the Bible is caricatured as a "gospel of gore" — as if in our world anybody could be squeamish about blood! Roads that avoid Calvary prove to go nowhere. There are no circuitous routes. The kingdom of God has a checkpoint and border control, and it is at the cross. Without having been to Calvary everybody lives a second-class existence as illegal immigrants. Passport and entry permits are repentance and faith in Christ Jesus. Then we may enter with the full privileges of citizens, no more "foreigners and aliens, but fellow citizens with God's people and members of God's household" (Eph. 2:19, NIV). The "covenants of promise" are ours.

We are not beggars asking the glorified saints to send us a few scraps of help. We don't need to collect their bones, hoping some of their holiness or grace will brush off on us and stand to our credit. Believers are not bone-pickers. If we do what the apostles did, we shall get what the apostles got from the same Father by the same Spirit on the same terms of grace.

The gifts are given to us freely. There are cheap imitations on the market: religious novelties, vibrations, spirit-powers, healing sunbeams and sweetness and light from nowhere in particular. In many countries our work disturbs those who have their own claims to power, protection and healing.

I recall an especially powerful witch being brought over from America to cast a spell and destroy what I was preaching. She stood at the back of the crowd and went through her performance. I wore the whole armor of God, as she attempted to launch a spiritual attack against me. Her attempt was futile against a blood-bought child of God.

But the Holy Spirit waits at the cross, and those who kneel at that altar, and there alone, receive His limitless blessings. At Calvary there are benefits far beyond the labored results of mantras, New Age processes and occultism. These are "the weak and beggarly elements" that Paul described in Galatians 4:8-11.

Now we shall see how real and how great His gifts are.

5

GOLDEN RULES OF THE GIFTS

My purpose in writing this book is not to intrigue readers but to emphasize that the gifts have a vital part to play in world evangelism. They are weapons of war, not toys to be played with. Mark 16:17-20 firmly ties miracles to the Great Commission.

Since this book is for those wanting practical knowledge, it will be helpful to quote a few facts. There are proofs of the link between bringing the gospel to the world and the gifts of Pentecost — true signs of the times, if we are not preoccupied with acquiring knowledge of prophetic signs and apocalyptic theories. One of these proofs is the widening gap between the genuine Christian life and the trends of wicked godlessness on the one hand, and the increasing action of the Holy Spirit worldwide on the other hand.

A survey of the American Assemblies of God published in 1989 (see Margaret Poloma, *Assemblies of God at the Crossroads*) revealed that six out of ten members had experienced a miraculous healing at some time; three out of four members experienced speaking in tongues, 83 percent regularly. Of even greater significance was the fact that those who spoke in tongues were the most active in evangelism and had the highest principles of holiness. Twice as many received salvation in places where the pastor strongly stressed the Pentecostal experience.[1]

The worldwide charismatic-Pentecostal movement illustrates this much more. From the original handful of "tongues-speakers," sitting on a few planks laid across nail kegs in a rundown area of Los Angeles in 1901, the revival has exceeded all previous religious growth and is likely to embrace 620 million believers by A.D. 2000. Largely because of the gifts, evangelical Christians are multiplying three times faster than the world population, with over 1.5 million full-time Christian workers.[2] This is by far the fastest growing faith in the world.

From the outset the church looked doomed, stillborn. To bring His message to the nations Jesus had only a few ordinary local men from Galilee. None of them demonstrated any brilliance or personal qualities that would make for success. In fact, they displayed a generous share of human failings. They were as unqualified for success as men ever could be. The Jewish leaders wrote them off as ignorant and unlearned. To meet the many outstanding intellectuals of their day, or even sway the semi-barbarous masses, these lowly fishermen and outcasts of Galilee possessed not even an inkling of educational or psychological know-how.

Their message seemed purposely unappealing. It had no element of intellectual wisdom, political promise or immediate social benefit. The worst part of all was that it centered on a leader from a seedy Galilean backwater town who ended up being executed as a common criminal.

Mission impossible? Against all expectations it became "mission accomplished." How? They advanced with a new secret. God personally worked with them with signs and wonders. More than that, He barbed their simple words with conviction and guided them to the hearts of hearers as unerringly and powerfully as David's stone was guided to the head of Goliath. Without personal charisma, the charisma of the Spirit of God clothed them. Their "secret"? The Holy Spirit.

Let us take it from there. If Christianity is to progress, this is the divine way. Christ knew that the world would expand. There are now sixty times more people alive than when He was here. He expected that all the world would hear His quiet words spoken so long ago in an obscure Roman province, not by normal propaganda methods, but by His power.

Because the world hovers between spiritual life and death, utmost consideration must be given to anything that can secure the destinies of precious people. What follows are principles of real importance. They may even be stressed by repeated mention throughout our chapters.

1. Just as in the wilderness Jesus was tempted to misuse divine powers when He had been filled with the Holy Spirit, so others are likely to be tempted in the same way.

The temptation springs from pride which corrupts our sincere motives for the power gifts and produces flamboyant behavior and egotistical display. Jesus was tempted to throw Himself off the pinnacle of the temple. One thing to be taken to heart is that the supernatural is not always sensational. We can attract personal admiration by our gifts, but our job is to set people's eyes on Jesus. When Paul and Barnabas were offered worship at Lystra they were horrified, running among the people to assert that they were not divinities.

Jesus said that this generation seeks a sign (Matt. 8:12). Sensation always has a market. We can exploit a situation and use the gifts of God for our own advantage. Simon Magus wanted the Holy Spirit in order to bolster his prestige (Acts 8:9,19). Uzza died for his presumption in putting his hand upon the ark of testimony (1 Chron. 13:10). If anyone says, "I would like the gift of healing," or some other gift, the proper response is, "Why?" Motive is vital.

2. The gifts of the Spirit do not confirm anybody's methods or theology. They operate by faith in God, not faith in a specific theory. They are not channeled through any doctrine except that of redemption. The Holy Spirit aims to glorify the crucified Christ. Testimonies that this formula or that formula have brought success are always to be found, but they do not prove what they are supposed to prove. God's mercies are "broader than the measures of our mind."[3] There is only one secret — faith. "This is the victory that has overcome the world — our faith" (l John 5:4). New techniques and highly publicized methods may seem to bring results, but in actuality they do not. God separates techniques and methods from the faith and responds only to faith.

In the New Testament whenever healings and miracles are attributed to anything at all, they are invariably attributed to faith. Otherwise it is the sovereign action of God. "Your faith has made you well. Go in peace," Jesus said to the woman with a hemorrhage (Luke 8:48). Her "method" could not have been more simple and childlike. Those seeking healing can be helped by being taught but the essential miracle ingredient is still simple, trusting faith in Jesus. That is all God bothers about, no matter what notions or innovations might occupy our muddled brains.

3. Gifts come with opportunity. They are issued to workers as they clock in at the door. Like modern technology, God's work needs specialized equipment, but it is found "on the job." He does not give it to us to keep handy in case we can use it sometime somewhere.

The need of the healing gift arises when we are moved by the plight of sufferers. That is when the gift operates. Jesus was moved with compassion. The word used here, splanknizomai, means "one's deepest innermost feelings of love and affection." When you are moved with compassion you have to blink tears away at the sight of people who are miserable and depressed with afflictions and ailments; you feel like screaming in protest at their condition. Go ahead; God will give all you need.

4. Gifts do not come secondhand. It is the prerogative of the Spirit alone to bestow them. Many have presumed to give gifts to other believers, but it has usually led to disappointment — miracle powers have not followed. We have not heard of any outstanding ministry produced by such attempts at transference.

I would like to give some guidance on meetings held to teach gifts. Teaching about gifts is good, but trying to receive gifts purely by being taught how to do things is no more possible than acquiring a musical or artistic gift by head learning.

But where faith and true desire are in our hearts, a true gift may be bestowed by the Spirit at any time. It may happen when people are listening eagerly to explanations about the *charismata*. But it is by the will of the Holy Spirit, not man's will. Be assured that while the Spirit completely ignores the pretentious "giftings" of the will of men, He does not ignore true openness and prayer. We can pray humbly for one another that we may be equipped for the work.

Paul himself asked for prayer that he might open his mouth boldly because the door of opportunity was there (1 Cor. 16:9; Eph. 6:19; Col. 4:3). The point to learn in those verses is that when the opportunity arose, Paul sought prayer help from everybody.

Perhaps we should take a few minutes to examine Scripture passages which have been offered as grounds for giftings. As a preliminary, we mention the fact that no Scripture verse gives instructions or commands for the practice. There are at best no more than ambiguous inferences.

The apostle Paul wrote in Romans 1:11, "I long to see you, that I may impart to you some spiritual gift [*charisma*], so that you may be established." What is that *charisma*? He tells us — "that is, that I may be encouraged together with you by the mutual faith both of you and me" (v. 12).

"This verse does not apply," says Siegfried Schatzmann, "for it has not the same technical sense of 'gift' as in 1 Corinthians 12."[4] It must be taken in context. Many *charismata* (gifts) are mentioned by Paul which are not miraculous endowments for believers. Indeed, the whole Christian faith consists of *charismata*, from salvation to sanctification.

It is quite clear, however, that Paul in Romans 1:11 is not thinking of giving an individual a "gift," for he is addressing the whole body of believers at Rome. He was not traveling all the way to Rome to bestow a gift of wisdom or discernment upon one man or woman, but, as he says, to establish the whole church.

Other verses are 1 Timothy 4:14 and 2 Timothy 1:6. Paul told Timothy "not [to] neglect" and "to stir up" the gift *(charisma)* given him by the laying on of Paul's hands and of those of the eldership. Was this a gift as in 1 Corinthians 12:8-10? If so, how could he "stir it up"? We are actually told what this gifting was, namely "a spirit of power, not timidity, and of love and self-discipline" (2 Tim. 1:7). The gifting by the elders was for his general ministry as a young Christian worker.

5. God gives whatever we need when we obey His call to service. When Timothy was thrust into a difficult task, Paul prayed for and laid hands upon him with other elders, and God blessed Timothy for the work, a normal procedure. A precisely similar situation is found in Acts 13:1-3. They laid hands on Paul and Barnabas to "separate" them for the work to which God had already called them. No gifting was attempted, but the laying on of hands was more than a ritual; it identified a need for strength from God. One can hardly suppose anybody would choose one gift of the nine listed in 1 Corinthians 12 for a young fellow left alone in a pagan world with a small company of believers, as if it were a going-away present. I cannot imagine which one they would choose for the big task that lay ahead of Timothy; but a general pastoral gifting — yes.

Another scripture passage quoted for gifting is 2 Kings 2:9 where Elisha asked Elijah to give him a double portion of his spirit. Elijah said it was a hard thing but promised it would be so if Elisha saw Elijah when he was taken from him. There are several points to note here.

God had already called Elisha to take the place of Elijah. He was his spiritual heir. This is what is meant when Elisha asked for "a double portion of your spirit." This did not mean twice as much power, though he did work twice as many miracles as Elijah. A "double portion" was the elder son's share of an inheritance as against other sons. Elijah was Elisha's spiritual father.

Elijah had been commanded by God to anoint Elisha but had not done so. This being the command of the Spirit, it made a special gifting necessary, because Elijah had not anointed him in the way that Moses had laid his hands upon the elders by specific divine mandate.

Elijah did not lay hands upon Elisha. The gifts of God's Spirit came to Elisha after Elijah had gone, when he took up the prophet's fallen mantle. God showed He was independent of Elijah.

When the call of God already rests upon a man's soul, which was the case with Elisha (1 Kin. 19:16), and as Elijah passes from the scene, God lets the same mantle fall on other shoulders. It is of God when such men come together. It has happened again and again.

These are the main Scripture passages used for gifting (as practiced originally by the Latter Rain Movement of the 1940s and 1950s). To attempt to direct the Holy Spirit seems to me to stretch Christian rights to the edge, close to usurping the sovereign prerogative of God. The definitive New Testament chapters concerning spiritual gifts — 1 Corinthians 12 to 14 — tell us to desire gifts, especially to prophesy, but they never suggest that gifts can be conferred by one person upon another, as we would expect if that was how God meant it to be.

Instead, the stress is laid first on people "desiring" (1 Cor. 14:1), "seeking" (v. 12) and "praying" (v. 13), but never that one should pray for another to receive. What is stated in 1 Corinthians 12:11 is that the Spirit apportions "to each one individually...as He wills."

The Holy Spirit does not wait for the church to take the initiative as to who should be gifted. The Lord has not committed Himself to empower those whom the church appoints. If a church must choose, then the New Testament model is for men already full of faith and the Holy Spirit (Acts 6:3, 5). Obviously God does not use unsuitable personalities, like warriors to be nursemaids or musicians to clean bricks, but God has His own ideas as to what He can do with people. He doesn't wait to see how church ballots go.

Church leaders should have the eye of discernment for the gifting of individuals by God and should encourage them, giving them the place for which they are fitted. Too often jealousy has actually arisen at others' gifts, and rather than opportunity being given them, they have been ignored and left to do other work. To the eternal credit of the leaders at Antioch, there was no jealousy; they released Paul who would go on to influence the entire world with the gospel.

The Bible never calls natural abilities *charismata*. Art, music, poetry, business acumen, linguistics, physical beauty and intellectual keenness are all assets which can be offered to God. Our skills may indeed be enhanced in God's service, but they still remain abilities and not *charismata*. The true *charismata* are the gifts of the Spirit given even to those who are disadvantaged from birth.

Unfortunately, too often churches and movements "hold men's persons in admiration" (see Jude 16, KJV) if they look good, have the right accent and, as James says in James 2:2, wear a gold ring and fine clothes. When Samuel was sent to anoint a new king, he looked admiringly on the impressive stature and personality of all of Jesse's sons except David, that brash youngster minding sheep. He didn't have the right-shaped head for a crown nor hand for a scepter — only a shepherd's staff. Yet this fresh-faced youngster, God said, was a man after His own heart (1 Sam. 13:14).

We discover our gifts best by working. The advice to "find your gift and use it" may have some wisdom in it, for to hide one's abilities is neglect. Sloth may be disguised as humility. The parable of the talents recognizes no excuse. Unused capacities must be uncovered and recovered.

Scripture, however, has better advice beyond finding one's gift. Paul said, "I can do all things through Christ who strengthens me" (Phil. 4:13). Finding your gift can be an excuse for doing nothing. Many say, "I have no gift." But the truly gifted are those with no natural abilities who are prepared to get up and go. The soldier brothers of David mocked him, suggesting he was no figure for the battlefield — shepherding was his lot. But his faith and anointing overcame all inexperience and deficiencies. God teaches a man to fight who does fight.

For the scriptural principle we turn to 1 Samuel 10:6-7: "The Spirit of the Lord will come upon you in power...and you will be changed into a different person. Do whatever your hand finds to do, for God is with you" (NIV). As the writer of Ecclesiastes observes, "God favors what you do" (Eccl. 9:7, NIV).

The gifts are a function of divine love and are performed best by the self-effacing believer. Chapters 12 and 14 of 1 Corinthians pivot on the central passage of love in Chapter 13. Scholars say that the key words of the Corinthian epistle are "word" and "deed" *(logos* and *ergon),* but, in fact, the keyword is "love." Paul's love touches every word and every deed in the epistle. A critical theologian has tried to show that Paul was recommending his own love-merits in that chapter.[5] Perhaps he was, but why not? He was supposed to be an example, and indeed he was.

The gifts are not for the perfect, despite what is said in the previous section. Who is the ideal Christian? Life is a continuing demonstration of our inconsistent efforts to reach perfection. But the gifts are *charismata* — the favors of grace, not certificates of merit. The book of Numbers, where Israel is exhibited for its failures, is perhaps the prime Bible lesson on this subject. They all failed, sometimes grossly, including the noble triad of Moses, Aaron and Miriam, and even Aaron's sons. Turn to the strange episode of Balaam in Numbers 22-24. When he tried to curse Israel, he could not. He found out why when God allowed him to see Israel as He saw them. He declared, "He has not observed iniquity in Jacob, nor has He seen wickedness in Israel" (Num. 23:21).

Is there a price to pay for the gifts? If there were, they would not be gifts, but purchases. Nevertheless, there may well be a price to pay in their use, to serve God with them. Those not prepared to risk their leisure, comfort, reputation and perhaps much more may be little used by God — even if He does bestow His powererful gifts upon them. A complete tool kit may be a marvelous gift for a carpenter, but it would be useless without the sweat of his brow. Gifts call for commitment. As Romans 12:7 puts it, "Let us use it in our ministering." His life is poured out with ours. Gifts are for givers. To get, give!

What are the best gifts? I think we should ask instead whether tongues is the least gift. Can it be brushed aside or even "swept under the carpet" as if it had no particular value? The answer is that if God sees fit to give it, then for us to despise it would be arrogance. The real worth of any gift is in the intention of the Giver and not what we may see as its practical usefulness. Gold has little practical use, but it is a standard of all treasure.

It really is time that the much quoted 1 Corinthians 12:31, "Covet earnestly the best gifts" (KJV), was retranslated. The word *covet* here is literally "desire eagerly" or "seek eagerly." Anybody can see that this can be taken in two ways: either that people are already seeking or that they are exhorted to seek. In the original Greek it can be either — that is, either active indicative (doing something continuously) or imperative (command). But we know from 1 Corinthians 14:12 that Paul is not telling them to seek the best gifts, for he knows "you are zealous for spiritual gifts." He would not tell them to do what they are already doing. The verse is in the indicative — they were seeking the best gifts. In fact, it wouldn't do if they all had them. "If the whole body were an eye, where would be the hearing?" (1 Cor. 12:17). Paul is evidently uneasy about what they considered to be the best gifts.

We are told to desire gifts (1 Cor. 14:1), of course, but not to seek the "best" gifts. That is another matter. What is actually said should be put together like this: "You covet earnestly the best gifts, and yet I show you a way of excellence" (Greek *meizona*, "best"). Then Paul uses the same word for excellence: "Now abide faith, hope, love, these three; but the greatest [*meizon*] of these is love. Pursue love, and desire spiritual gifts" (1 Cor. 13:13–14:1).

The value of any gift depends on the situation. A monkey wrench in the garden is less useful than a lawn mower. The power to heal is of no value among the young and healthy, but discernment probably could be. Some have suggested that Paul names the gifts in descending order of value. But they cannot support this assertion with Scripture. In fact, gifts that come first in the original list are not named at all in the next list in the same chapter. He especially encourages the Corinthians to seek prophecy, but it is sixth in the second list.

The gift lists never mention every gift, and they usually leave out some mentioned elsewhere. This suggests that there are other unlimited possibilities in the Holy Spirit. The casting out of demons is not mentioned nor the convicting of sinners. The idea that we must have a prior Bible instance for every manifestation is itself not a biblical principle. No such idea is mentioned; otherwise what use is the spirit of discernment? There is a vast range of supernatural phenomena, and God does not limit Himself to precedent.

Let me specify. Strange things took place in the classical revivals which are not found in the New Testament. They are never questioned. Instead, they are usually taken as strong evidences of God at work. For that matter, classical revival itself has no parallel in Scripture. The Holy Spirit has never tied Himself down. We should never assume that those revivals are the way He will work forever. He never works contrary to the Bible, of course. For example, there may be minimal scriptural examples of believers being "slain in the Spirit" as some call it; but through the centuries it has been seen as an act of God. It does not contradict any revelation about the activity of God. Of course, like the Egyptian sorcerers with Moses, what God does can be counterfeited and simulated, but that does not invalidate what is genuine.

The guidance of Paul in 1 Corinthians regarding the gifts is not to be taken as the law of Mount Sinai. For example, 1 Corinthians 14:27 and 29 say, "If anyone speaks in a tongue, two — or at the most three — should speak, one at a time, and someone must interpret...Two or three prophets should speak, and the others should weigh carefully what is said" (NIV). These imperatives have been treated as law. Pastors have sternly rebuked a fourth utterance and declared it to be "not of God" and "in the flesh." Churches have split because of the public humiliation of a sincere member making a fourth utterance. Presumably, if the benediction had been pronounced and a second meeting begun, the tongues five minutes later would have been in order! Damage done by a grace-less legal ruling is far greater than any damage that a fourth message could do.

If the whole of Paul's teaching is taken to heart, that kind of legalism would be impossible. All his rulings, whether on the gifts or on anything else, must be seen in a framework of grace. Of course, we are to take all moral laws in the Bible with utter seri-ousness. But the gifts are another matter. They spring from life in the Spirit, a lively, powerful, manifesting activity. To box in the bubbling dynamic of the Spirit with cast-iron regulations is insensitive and incompatible with the free energies of the Spirit.

Paul was faced with the runaway and exuberant "non-wisdom" of Christians who had just come out of heathenism and had little experience or written Scripture to guide them. How can we today be led of the Spirit while the whip of the law is cracked behind us? "Where the Spirit of the Lord is, there is liberty" (2 Cor. 3:17).

These principles will reappear as we proceed with this compre-hensive examination.

6

WORDS OF THE WORD

Every subject has to have its special words, jargon or code words to avoid repetition. I know people want a simple gospel, but to "grow in the grace and knowledge of our Lord and Savior Jesus Christ" (2 Pet. 3:18) without learning anything is impossible. Jesus said, "If you abide in Me, and My words abide in you, you will ask what you desire, and it shall be done for you" (John 15:7). There are two vital conditions for prayer — abiding in Christ and His words abiding in us. To grasp the biblical meaning of this and other scriptural words then is important. The Bible makes the rules for studying the Bible. We will follow that truth now.

We should begin with an expression mentioned frequently in

this book: spiritual. To describe somebody as "very spiritual" tells us a lot about them. Some Corinthians called themselves spiritual, but they didn't mean what we mean nor what Paul meant either. Paul was doubtful of them, as he shows in 1 Corinthians 14:37 — "If anyone thinks himself to be…spiritual…." These spiritual men had perhaps been associated with the mystery religions. Many claimed secret and esoteric experiences or had been initiated. They were spiritual in the pagan or occult sense.

Paul gave *spiritual* a Christian meaning — a person filled with the Holy Spirit walking in obedience and righteousness, not in the pride and lusts of the flesh. He refers to true and false spirituality in 1 Corinthians 12:1-7. One of the tests there is that true spirituality produces something for "the common good" (v. 7, NIV) or, as the King James Version puts it, for "every man to profit withal." That is a principle which applies to all the gifts.

Spiritual Gifts

It was Paul's idea to talk about spiritual gifts. The Corinthians had not asked Paul about them because they thought they knew all that was to be known. But it didn't leave Paul very happy. He said in 1 Corinthians 12:1, "Concerning spiritual gifts, brethren, I do not want you to be ignorant," which he judged they were. He goes on to say in 1 Corinthians 14:38, "If anyone is ignorant, let him be ignorant," meaning that if they still thought they knew it all and didn't accept correction of their ideas, then they would stay ignorant. They had been "carried away" with their previous knowledge, which was similar but belonged to "dumb idols" (12:2). The Greeks were famous for learning, but the things of the Spirit are different. A university doctorate in social sciences or physics doesn't make one wise in the things of God. Gaining spiritual knowledge is like taking fire into one's soul, not just hoarding cold facts in one's head.

This is our major subject, so we will take a closer look at what spiritual gifts are called. First, we should know that chapter 12 is really about the church. The teaching on spiritual gifts is incidental.

The Corinthians had written asking for help, and Paul had dealt with several matters that troubled them. Sadly, some things they should have worried about did not trouble them. They allowed factions to arise which divided the fellowship in Corinth; to Paul that was a very alarming situation. But they also misused the gifts. Paul now points out these matters and relates both problems together. The result is this truly marvelous exposition which he has left us.

Our English versions use the term "spiritual gifts" (1 Cor. 12:1). Now the original word in Greek really has nothing to do with "gift." It is *pneumatika* (from *pneuma* — spirit), found twenty-six times in the New Testament. This special word is translated "spiritual gift(s)" only ten times, but more often as spiritual men, a spiritual law, meat, rock, body, songs, a house and so on. In Romans 1:11 Paul wanted to impart a *pneumatikon* to the Romans, meaning "something spiritual," a benefit. The proper word in Greek for "gift" is actually not used in 1 Corinthians 12-14, except twice incidentally. The Corinthians liked the word *pneumatika* — it was their word. But Paul coined a special word which he preferred — *charisma*. Once again he avoids the normal word for "gift" *(doron)* and chooses the word *charisma* which is so well known today. It means "a favor." It is surprising that Paul doesn't use a straightforward "gift" word, but we shall see why.

Paul was the apostle of grace *(charis* and *charisma)*. He introduced it into the Christian vocabulary. It belongs to a group of words like *chairo*, "to rejoice," and *chara*, "joy." There are some wonderful texts using *charisma*. In 2 Corinthians 9:14 we read of "the exceeding grace [*charis*] of God in you." That is, we are marked with "exceeding favor" from God. Paul uses the proper word for "gift" *(doron)* only for an outright gift, something given to hold. For example, verse 15 goes on to say, "Thanks be to God for His indescribable gift!" *(doron)*. That outright personal gift was God's Son, Jesus, and He is ours forever. In John 3:16 we have the same kind of giving: "God so loved the world that He gave [*dokeo*] His only begotten Son." Jesus is God's *doron* to us.

Grace is *charis*. It stands for God's gracious attitude. The Old Testament talks about God turning His face toward us, showing the light of a favorable countenance. That is what grace really is — a kindly attitude, not a power, force or substance. For many centuries the old theologians spoke as if grace were something measurable. Later, others thought of grace as a strange power ("amazing grace") that came upon people in an unpredictable way. They confused grace with the Holy Spirit. Even now, many believe that there are saints who have accumulated large quantities of grace by their virtue — enough for themselves and for others, as a kind of spiritual treasury. Others believe that the way to obtain grace is through the sacraments by which people can gather grace to their spiritual credit account. But an abstract quality can't be saved up.

However, the wonderful thing is that although God's grace refers to His attitude toward us, it is never abstract in Scripture. It always has a concrete form. Grace is in His deeds and gifts. It is the only way we know His grace, by His practical demonstration of it. So the word *grace* has come to stand for something tangible, good and real. The greatest *charis* of all is Jesus Christ, "the indescribable gift." He is grace personified, embodied. A lovely use of *charis* comes in Ephesians 4:7. We read that we are "given grace," where the two words for giving and for grace come together *(edothe charis)*.

Now all "spiritual gifts" *(pneumatika)* are also *charismata*. In fact, every gift from God is a grace gift, a *charisma*, but not all grace gifts are miracle gifts; that is, not all *charisma* are *pneumatika*. Even the sunshine and rain are acts of grace, for as Jesus said, "He makes His sun rise on the evil and on the good, and sends rain on the just and on the unjust" (Matt. 5:45). God is the God of grace — that is His character, and that is the God with whom we have to do. Only on the grounds of His grace can we approach Him. We earn nothing that He gives us — certainly not the spiritual gifts. Everything we have is a demonstration of His smiling goodness of heart toward us — food, sunshine, breath and so on. Don't grumble about wet weather — the rain is a *doron* of God!

The ordinary words of giving are found 416 times in the New Testament [1], but — take special note — only twice in 1 Corinthians 12-14. One of these uses is in 1 Corinthians 12:7 where it says we are given the "manifestation" of the Spirit. The same kind of total giving is spoken of in Ephesians 4:8-11 when God gives apostles, prophets, teachers and so on — straightforward gifts *(edoke domata)*. But whether God gives in that sense, or in any other way, it is still a grace gift, a *charisma*.

It is wonderful to know that grace itself is completely free. We don't have to curry favor with God by any kind of behavior that might impress Him. He loves us just as we are. Grace is there all the time — like the air we breathe — not just occasionally. Another lovely example of a real gift by grace is in Romans 5:15, "the gift by grace" *(hedorea enchariti)*, which means grace is a real and permanent gift to us.

Nowadays, of course, everybody uses the word *charisma*. They talk about a charismatic leader or somebody with charisma — that is, with personality. It was introduced into modern language by Max Weber, a German professor, one of the founders of sociology during this century. He turned it into his jargon word for leadership qualities. Leadership, however, is not what Paul was talking about.

There is still something else that we might be confused about. The gifts of the Spirit never designate natural talents, such as a gift for music or art. Natural talents are our own abilities to use as we like, for good or evil. The gifts in 1 Corinthians 12 are supernatural manifestations of the Spirit. They only operate according to God's will as the Spirit "gives utterance." Our will to use them depends on His will and His timing.

Before we go any further I must explain why gifts have to differ from person to person. Paul shows there are all kinds of members with different gifts. He mentions a few of those in the first list: miracles, healings, tongues and interpretation. Then he brings in another order of gifts — people: apostles, prophets, teachers, helper, administrators. These various classes of gifts are all *charismata*, but different. Not everybody has the same part to play, yet all are equally important.

He speaks about the body having "less honorable" members (1 Cor. 12:23) which receive less admiration. He does not specify our "less honorable members" physically, but he does list some members of Christ who get little mention, particularly helpers and administrators. Feet don't get the same attention as faces. Paul adjusts that and places "helps" alongside the most eminent appointments, such as apostles, and on the same level as the mighty manifestations and gifts most highly valued by the Corinthians, such as tongues, interpretation and miracles.

Paul is using the same principle as Jesus, who Himself said, "He who receives a prophet in the name of a prophet shall receive a prophet's reward" (Matt. 10:41). Note that He did not say "in My name," but "in the name of a prophet." It means that to accept a prophet as a prophet, helping him, showing that you would do a prophet's work if you could, will bring you a reward equal to the prophet's reward. It is faithfulness in service that counts. One service does not outrank another. Christ became a servant to His

servants and washed the disciples' feet, an act for which no supernatural powers are needed.

There is no such thing as greater and lesser gifts. A *pneu-matikon* is from God and therefore cannot be trivial. So many want
to belittle tongues or despise them as no more than a peculiar psy-
chological phenomenon or something arising from a deeper part of
the mind which we can't control. Those experiencing the tongues
know that it is nothing of the kind, and they are the only ones who
can judge. "He who is spiritual judges all things" (1 Cor. 2:15).
Those seeking the best gifts — like the Corinthians — would do
well to remember that we are never told to seek the best gifts. That
is misreading the Word of God. All the *pneumatika* are favors of
God, and all are to be equally valued.

Manifestation

"To each one the manifestation of the Spirit is given for the
common good" (1 Cor. 12:7, NIV). The Greek word *phaneroo* is
nearly always translated "manifest," once or twice as "appear" or
"show," and it means "to show openly." The Holy Spirit shows
Himself.

You will notice that in 1 Corinthians 12 Paul speaks mainly
about the Spirit Himself and the body of Christ. He is emphasizing who the Spirit really is and how we should distinguish the Holy
Spirit from false spirits. He lists the gifts in order to show who is
behind them — the "same Spirit." Whether it is tongues, interpretation, discernment or anything else, it is the Holy Spirit showing
Himself: God in action. In chapter 14, of course, he gives much
more attention to the gifts. So a word of knowledge is a manifestation of the Spirit. That is what is given — a manifestation and
not a permanent ability.

Speaking by the Spirit of God, nobody calls Jesus "accursed" (see 1 Cor. 12:3). Outside Christianity, ecstatic speech is demonic, and demons never glorify Jesus. There are different sources of supernatural phenomena. Spirits may manifest themselves and imitate the works and gifts of God.

Some have suggested that because speaking with tongues is heard among non-Christians, such as Spiritualists and Buddhists, all who speak with tongues are of the devil. One Pentecostal historian said that when Buddhists and others spoke with tongues it would be the same thing as Joel spoke about, God pouring out His Spirit upon all flesh! It does not follow that if a Spiritualist speaks with tongues, then everybody who speaks with tongues is a Spiritualist. We may as well say that because burglars use a steel jimmy, everybody who uses a steel jimmy is a burglar. The fact that there is a counterfeit should not lead us to reject the genuine.

Wisdom, knowledge, healings, tongues and so on are manifestations but not *dorons*. They are actions of the Spirit, and an action cannot be a gift. The gift of music is not an action but an independent ability. The "gift," as we call it, simply means that one certain individual is often used by the Spirit in a particular manner, such as prophecy or miracles. This will be clear when we look at each gift in turn.

"Holy Spirit" and "the Holy Spirit"

The Spirit behind these gifts is the same Spirit as in Genesis 1:2 who hovered over the face of the deep. Sometimes in the original texts we read of "the Holy Spirit" and sometimes just "Holy Spirit" without the definite article. Does this matter? Don't we ourselves sometimes speak of "the Holy Spirit" and sometimes a "Holy Spirit meeting" or a "Holy Spirit gift"?

The difference is really a blessing to understand. Whenever we read "the Holy Spirit," the Spirit Himself is referred to. It names

Him as a person. When it is just "Holy Spirit," it is something He does out of Himself, a manifestation. In Joel 2:28 we read that God will "pour out His Spirit" — out of Him, some of Him. However, the wonderful thing to note is this: What the Holy Spirit does is of Himself — He pours Himself out, and each gift is a manifestation of Himself. The power of the Spirit *is* the Spirit, not some other power He makes. We human beings cannot pour ourselves out. We can give our time or effort, but the Spirit Himself fills us. He is "given" *(doron)*, an abiding gift, His powerful presence within us. Jesus said, "You will receive power when the Holy Spirit comes on you" (Acts 1:8, NIV).

His power is not an impersonal force which we can play with. Power is the Spirit, God in action, the same awesome personal force that created the heavens and the earth. To say to people, "Have some more Holy Spirit," or "I am giving you more anointing," is flippant. We can't offer people a bottle of God. The Spirit is not a spiritual stockpile for evangelists or teachers to hand out as they fancy.

There is also no power of grace distinct from the Holy Spirit. The Holy Spirit is Himself a generating force. He generates us (John 3:3). We cannot generate power, for it is the Holy Spirit. The Holy Spirit cannot be generated by prayer, holiness, obedience or any of the techniques and formulas now on the church market. God is not an energy capable of manufacture by using the right spiritual technique. To speak of getting twice as much power by twice as much prayer is a wrong idea. We are talking about a person. The power of God is channeled through the Word of God.

First Corinthians 12:4 says, "There are diversities of gifts, but the same Spirit." The word "diversities" *(diaireseis)* is used widely for many different things. Paul is drawing a sharp contrast between the variety of gifts and workings and the absolute single identity of the Holy Spirit. In the pagan temples and oracles of Paul's day each separate god, such as Diana of the Ephesians, had his or her temple, and the spirit of that god was supposed to operate there.

Some think it doesn't matter, that all spirits belong to a common area of spirit, the spirit world. Outside the Christian faith various religions have their techniques for tapping the spirit world, some by mantras, some by spirit guides, some by incantations or witchcraft practices, verbal formulas or magic words. The contemplatives and mystics tune in to the vibrations, voices and forces to connect with this area of spirit. New Age takes in all of these methods.

But God does not belong to any realm of spirit. He is above all gods, above all spirits, the wholly other one. He is not to be compared with any spirit power. Buddhists, Zen, the Soka Gakkai and many New Age cults claim to draw upon some mass force, such as cosmic power, or the earth spirit.

Against all this the Bible brings the stark and searing light of truth — the truth that the Son of God, Jesus, by whose word all things were made, is above all principalities and powers and every name that can be named. He gives the Holy Spirit when we ask, without secret techniques or word power. There is no formula, only trust and love. The mighty One is not to jump at our bidding to perform wonders when we utter the right words of command, like a pet animal. God is not a genie, a slave of the lamp.

Warnings in Scripture about counterfeit signs and wonders should be taken seriously. Satan has not retired from his work (1 John 4:1). On the other hand, the genuine believer trusting in Jesus Christ who shed His blood for us is perfectly safe and need not fear that a scorpion spirit will be given him if he asks for the Holy Spirit (Luke 11:12). Believers are children of the kingdom. The first duty of a state is defense of the realm and the security of those within it. God is our salvation. We in Christ are "dwellers in Zion," whose bulwarks and walls are impregnable. No marauding spirit can penetrate through to us. There is peace within its walls.

"For the Common Good"

Almost all of chapter 12 of 1 Corinthians concerns the church, and the gifts are for the common good of all members. The church is Paul's constant concern. He was the "steward of the mystery" (see 1 Cor. 4:1) of the church and of the amazing revelation of God's new creation which was not built by getting like-minded folk together but which depends upon human differences, different gifts and different people. Furthermore, in Christ those differing personalities created in Christ Jesus are brought to the highest development of distinction in harmonious interplay.

The modern tendency is to depersonalize and reduce us to a few personality types. The world's idea is the club, a class of people with their mutual similarities and subtle marks. God's idea is the church. The first thing God does is break down these walls of partition and makes each person a class on his or her own, a person in his or her own right. A body needs eyes which are totally different from hair or nails, and the church is "the body of Christ" depending on the unique differences of members to complete it.

The great social and political schemes usually attempt to make us all even, to put us all in some common class — like ants — or even dress us all alike, as Chairman Mao's Chinese masses used to do, with no cohesion unless each unit is molded to the same pattern, like bricks in a wall. But God does not mold bricks, rather "living stones," each uniquely sculptured. The world sees distinctions as weaknesses, but God sees them as strengths. Weakness through uniformity, but strength through unity.

Spiritual gifts are supplemented by the gifts of apostles, pastors, prophets, teachers and evangelists (Eph. 4:11). They are as different as chalk and cheese, yet they are brought together by divine chemistry creating an indissoluble bond.

The whole book of 1 Corinthians is really about this unity.

The Corinthians recognized differences between Paul, Peter and Apollos and attached themselves to one name or another as cult figures. Each group vied with the others to be the chief party, hoping to make all members followers of their particular cult figure. This attempt at sameness led to division. It was an ecumenical effort, and it failed. Churches are supposed to be different, like the people in them, but all are one in Christ.

In the interest of ecumenical unity, whole denominations have denied their own history and compromised the very principles for which they existed. Being different is no sin. The expression "the common good" (NIV) in 1 Corinthians 12:7 is the Greek word *sumpheron*, from which comes the word *symphony*. The Spirit is like a composer conducting his own work, bringing counterpoint and harmony from many interlocking themes and instruments, not from everyone playing the same tune.

The Threefold Work of the Trinity

Having made ourselves familiar with some of the language about the Spirit and the gifts, we will end this section with the words in 1 Corinthians 12:4-6:

> There are different kinds of gifts, but the same Spirit.
> There are different kinds of service, but the same Lord.
> There are different kinds of working, but the same God
> works all of them in all men.

Gifts, service and workings: all different. Then it says, "the same Spirit...Lord...God" — different names, but showing the same God. It is rather striking that when Paul is stressing that the same Spirit is behind the gifts he uses three different names for God.

Why is that? To show again that the most perfect unity of all, that of the Godhead, embraces differences. Gifts by the Spirit, service by the Lord, workings by God. Three operations by three persons in the Godhead, but one great work. The unity of the Spirit is complex. God is a complex Being — the trinity. And so is the church. It is rich with all the poetic inventiveness of God. A pastor joked, "It takes all sorts to make a world, and I've got them all in my church." Of course! Why not?

I would like to explore this text a little more.

Gifts

They are many *(charismata).*

Service

It implies eagerness or readiness to serve *(diakonion).* The "blessed of my Father" in Matthew 25 did not know they had served the Son of man, Christ. What they had done was the result of their heart's spontaneous outflow. Many people feel they are doing so little or that they have no ability, knowledge or opportunity. But they are folk who stick to their church, and people like that make churches possible. What they do *is* who they are. The Holy Spirit is like that. He just is what He is — alive, active, moving, concerned. What His character is — that describes the Spirit who comes upon us. Those whom He anoints find something within them which moves them to serve eagerly and full of zest, faithful when they can do nothing.

Nobody should hold back or quench the Spirit by pretending to be humble and not wanting the limelight, or by doing nothing until they "feel led" — or forced.

Some people seem not to feel led as often as they ought to be or as often as would help a church. Too many people not feeling led makes a meeting feel like lead. Somebody said that the difference between early Christians and later ones is that the early ones felt led more often.

"The spirits of the prophets are subject to the prophets" (1 Cor. 14:32). We can quench the Spirit, or we can "fan into flame the gift of God," as Paul needed to say to Timothy (2 Tim. 1:6, NIV). The Spirit moves when we move. Holy Ghost meetings are supposed to flow with the supernatural. Every gift is a service. If we stick to Paul's words, all *pneumatika* (miracle gifts) and *charismata* (grace gifts) are *diakonia* (service), a bursting upward of the energy of the Spirit.

Workings

First Corinthians 12:10 used the Greek *energemata* to describe the activity or working of the Holy Spirit that calls forth miracles. The activity of the Holy Spirit moves us to work in the same way. We read in Scripture, "Your word has given me life" (Ps. 119:50), and that we "shall run and not be weary, [we] shall walk and not faint" (Is. 40:31). The word is different from the power *(dunamis)* promised in Acts. That is potential, power in reserve, like a stick of dynamite. It will just lie there, like stone. People pray for "the power" and receive it, no doubt, but maybe they should pray for the moving of the Spirit, for they just keep on praying for power without doing anything. The *dunamis* potency is directed to human need.

We can be like spiritual bodybuilders, developing ourselves for the sake of being strong. But what is the use of a man being able to lift three hundred pounds above his head in the gymnasium if he can't lift a finger to help his wife in the kitchen? What is the use of all our clamoring for power if we don't do the jobs that need to be done — the door-to-door evangelism, for example, or Sunday school work — and leave it all to the faithful few?

The release of the power of the Spirit is never possible while we remain inactive. When we apply ourselves to do the will of God in service, God sees us making ourselves an empty vessel for His Spirit. This is the real purpose of our studies together, to see the world church not merely full of power but full of energetic people. The same God who is behind speaking with tongues or healing is behind the "workings," the willing service to God.

Part Two

7

A Word of Wisdom

Wisdom and love are twins upon whose arms all the gifts should lean.

I t has been difficult to write this chapter about a word of wisdom without also dealing with the word of knowledge, since the two are complementary. But I will endeavor to deal with knowledge separately in the next chapter.

The gift of wisdom is the first in the 1 Corinthians 12 list. It is no more than a name, and it is neither defined nor explained. That is how the rest of the gifts are introduced also. Obviously, Paul assumed the Corinthians would know what he was talking about since he knew them. He did not know us, however, so for each gift we need to be sure of what he had in mind. In this instance, for example, wisdom has several forms, so which form of wisdom is the gift?

The golden rule in Bible interpretation is that which Paul himself laid down in this epistle, chapter 2, verses 12-13: "That we might know the things that have been freely given to us by God. These things we also speak, not in words which man's wisdom teaches but which the Holy Spirit teaches, comparing spiritual things with spiritual." "Spiritual things" here is the same word translated "spiritual gifts" in chapter 12:1 — *pneumatika*. Understanding the Bible is not a matter of guesswork. The Bible is its own interpreter.

Wisdom was a real field of interest among Jews and Gentiles alike; each had their tradition of wisdom which influenced the national outlook. The Greeks "sought after wisdom" (1 Cor. 1:22). They were the first nation to experience intellectual awakening. From Thales in the seventh century B.C. until the Christian era over seven hundred years later, the Greeks produced outstanding thinkers who tried to guide their countrymen in life. Their wisdom took many twists and turns; mind contradicted mind. A little light flickered in the darkness, but the day of full enlightenment never dawned for them, and so they continued the search for a convincing worldview. These pagan thinkers are still closely studied, but philosophy is as far away as ever from bringing a solid ground of hope to us all. Paul went to Athens, however, and preached Jesus (Acts 17:16-34), the first voice ever heard there that rang with a trumpet note of certainty and ultimate wisdom.

Jewish wisdom was entirely different from that of men like Socrates and Aristotle, and we shall come to that in due course.

First we must observe exactly what is said. Several translations, including the King James Version, render the phrase as "the word of wisdom." In Greek it is not "the word," but "a word;" that is, one of many words, not the word pointing to a word already in view, but a word as yet not known. A car is any car, but the car is the one being used. A word of wisdom is a new shaft of light thrown on a situation.

Looking at the four words again, the New English Bible translation is "the gift of wise speech." Again, this is not what the Greek actually says. E.H. Robertson also translates it "to speak with wisdom," and Weymouth says "the utterance of wisdom." These renderings suggest a general gift of always being able to speak wisely, like Solomon's gift. Solomon has often been used as an example of the gift of the word of wisdom, but that is not the same thing. Solomon's gift from God was general wisdom, which God's people can ask for according to James 1:5.

Here, however, we are looking at one of the supernatural gifts which occasionally brings a word of wisdom. It does not turn people into oracles with pearls of wisdom falling from their lips every time they open them. How long a word of wisdom may be in words is not stated, but a wise idea or truth could need anything from a sentence to a book for its expression. Whatever its form, we are to see it as being of the Holy Spirit; that is, supernatural — a manifestation, as this chapter explains. Examples of it abound in Scripture. Jesus, for instance, promised persecuted believers such words of wisdom. He told them not to think beforehand what to say when brought before the courts, for the Father would give them the words at that moment.

What Wisdom?

If there are various schools or species of wisdom, what sort of wisdom is covered by the word of wisdom? Are we just to brush the question aside and say, "Well — any kind"? That would hardly be "rightly dividing the word of truth" (2 Tim. 2:15). There is little question of the kind of wisdom to which Paul alluded. His mind at this time was moving in only one area of wisdom even while he wrote this epistle. He began with two chapters saying what wisdom is: It is wisdom "in Christ" — "Christ Jesus, who became for us wisdom from God" (1 Cor. 1:30). A word of wisdom would fall within that class of wisdom which is related to Christ.

We know a little more of Paul's ideas on the subject. His were molded by Scripture. The Old Testament is full of wisdom. One Hebrew word alone for wisdom occurs 140 times. In the New Testament a Greek word (*sophia*) appears 51 times, and it does not mean something different in 1 Corinthians from what it means generally in the New Testament.

Wisdom did in fact mean something different to the Corinthians, and that is why Paul spent so much of his letter putting their thoughts into a Christian perspective. The wisdom which affected the Corinthians was either the abstract philosophy of the Greeks or that of their mystery religions. The age of the great Greek philosophers and of men like the supreme sculptor Phidias was also a crude age of primitive ignorance, barbarity, superstition and vile devotion to the ancient gods. Apart from mathematics, Greek wisdom generally consisted only of statements of thought, and definitions.

Jewish wisdom was always practical — how to live. It was "understanding," something deeper than words, which touched the instincts of behavior. The Old Testament reflects this national feature. The Bible even personifies wisdom (see Proverbs 8). The same principle turned their thoughts of God to a practical vein. For the Greeks, God existed entirely as an abstract idea arrived at by reason and too remote to be reached. For the Jews God was a living presence among them, and they talked of Him in human terms as having hands, feet, arms and ears. Of course, Israel never thought God had actual physical parts, but they used this kind of language because He made man in His own image; our human limbs and parts are a material picture of God's infinitely greater spiritual reality. We have arms, but "You have a mighty arm," they said. The Jewish wisdom was always earthly. The Greeks were centuries behind Israel and spoke of God in impersonal terms, sometimes as no more than abstract good. The Greek god was faceless.

The longest book of wisdom debating God and life in Scripture is the book of Job. It is also the oldest book in the Bible. It faces the ultimate questions, but they are brought down to earth and revolve around the experience of Job. The talk is not academic, but factual and practical.

The book of Proverbs is a book of wisdom, but it also describes it in personal terms in chapters 8 and 9. "I am understanding" (8:14). Wisdom is not merely thought of as common sense, experience, good advice, acumen or skill; that is human thinking. It moves into another dimension. God comes into the picture. "The fear of the Lord is the beginning of wisdom" (Prov. 9:10). "Unwisdom" is the opposite: "The fool has said in his heart, 'There is no God' " (Ps. 14:1). The wisdom Paul preached was the same personal, practical, down-to-earth understanding. He drew his wisdom from the character of the living God of Israel. Of course, for Paul the wisdom of God was summed up in the revelation of God's Son incarnate, Jesus Christ. His "gift of wisdom" relates to that kind of understanding, as we shall see.

The word of wisdom is a matter of wisdom for living, not academic insight. But we should look closely at the Bible's remarkable definition: "The fear of the Lord is the beginning of wisdom, and the knowledge of the Holy One is understanding" (Prov. 9:10). That is a revolutionary statement — repeated often in the Old Testament — which cuts across both ancient and modern thought. No other nation or literature achieved such a radical conception. Wisdom is made to rest on faith in God as the rock of eternal truths. It is not subject to fashion, opinion, speculation or any academic school of thought. Amid the disturbing perplexities of life, the wisdom of God is the stabilizer.

The man who knows God in Christ has found wisdom. He

doesn't chase some unknown something, like the godless who seek without any idea of what they seek or how to recognize what they are looking for even if they were to find it. Secular progress has not yet decided what its goal is. Therefore, it can't know whether it is progressing or not — it might be going in the wrong direction all the time! Christian onlookers see the present world progress as a regression backward into the darkness, wondering and wandering. "The wisdom of their wise men shall perish" (Is. 29:14). Daniel said wisdom belongs to God and "God gives wisdom to the wise" (Dan. 2:21). For Christians, Jesus is the "wisdom of God" (1 Cor. 1:24) and "the way, the truth and the life" (John 14:6).

The wisdom literature — some of it in Bible books like Job, Psalms, Proverbs and Ecclesiastes — is a mass of garnered experience for successful living. Ecclesiastes, for instance, handles it in a most original way. On the surface Ecclesiastes is a cynic's book, saying the world doesn't make sense; it scoffs at everything in creation as vanity, or emptiness, using the word thirty-five times in reference to existence.[1] The same Hebrew word *(hebel)* is used to describe the nothingness of idols. How could such deeply religious people as the Jews include such a book together with Psalms which are rich with praises and thanks for God's creation?

The answer is that it balances the matter with another expression used thirty-one times — "under the sun." Ecclesiastes is "under-the-sun" thinking, limited to the horizons of this material world. The materialist outlook provides no answers and no logic and leaves mortal existence a riddle. If the world is the whole show, a closed order, a merry-go-round destined to wind down and stop, it is meaningless and should never have existed. We are then like a colony of ants busy in the closed world of a plastic museum showcase.

The world's wise try to make the best of a bad job. Paul Tillich, a pantheist, talked of the "courage to be" — be brave while you

back (from left to right):
Dario Navac
Anni Bonnke
Reinhard Bonnke
Jeannette Bonnke

front (from left to right):
Gabriele Navac with
Annika and Christopher
Susanne Urbanowicz (Bonnke)
Kai-Uwe Bonnke

CfaN headquarters in
Frankfurt, Germany
since 1987

Countries in which CfaN crusades have already been held

Countries in which a CfaN crusade has not yet been held

Tunisia
Morocco
Algeria
Libya
Egypt
Western Sahara
Mauritania
Mali
Niger
Chad
Sudan
Senegal
Gambia
Guinea-Bissau
Guinea
Burkina Faso
Benin
Nigeria
Ethiopia
Sierra Leone
Ivory Coast
Togo
Ghana
Liberia
Cameroon
Central African Republic
Equatorial Guinea
Uganda
Kenya
Somalia
Gabon
Congo
Rwanda
Burundi
Cabinda
Zaire
Tanzania
Angola
Malawi
Zambia
Mozambique
Namibia
Zimbabwe
Botswana
Madagascar
Swaziland
South Africa
Lesotho

CfaN

Almost 200,000 people in a single meeting in Nairobi, Kenya, in June 1988

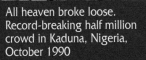

All heaven broke loose.
Record-breaking half million
crowd in Kaduna, Nigeria,
October 1990

Walking again after four years!
Jos, Nigeria, November 1989

Deaf and dumb since birth, now he
can hear and speak

05.000 people at the largest evangelistic crusade in Islamic Indonesia - Jakarta, May 1991

◄ Tens of thousands are baptized in the Holy Spirit.

Walking and leaping and ►
praising God!

"Launch out into the deep and let down your nets for a catch." (Luke 5:4, NKJV)
Campaign in Mbuji-Mayi, Zaire, draws crowds of up to 360,000 in August 1991

Great rejoicing as witchcraft items are burned

A campaign of "signs and wonders"!
Both Christian and Muslims were he

State President Joseph S. Momoh ca
to officially open the CfaN Gospel Cam
in Freetown, Sierra Leone, December

The people of Freetown, Sierra Leone, receive God's miracle power with rejoicing at the CfaN Gospel crusade in December 1991.

A blind woman rejoices in her newfound sight.

175,000 people crowded into the stadium in Kumasi, Ghana, April 1993

195,000 people heard the Gospel in Tanga, Tanzania, June 1993

Proclaiming the good news of Jesus Christ to 150,000 people in Madras, India, March 1994

And Jesus said, "Take up your bed, and go your way." (Mark 2:11, NKJV) Paralytic walks in Bujumbura, Burundi, August 1989.

After ten years of total blindness, he sees again. Bangui, C.A.R., Februray 1992

Jubilation as in Bible days during the Gospel crusade in Goma, Zaire, June 1990 exist, for you will vanish one day! Life is just a one-shot try. "Human life begins on the far side of despair," said a modern unbeliever. This agrees with the despair of godless philosophers like Camus, Russell and Ayer. The "under-the-sun" attitude is the heart of idolatry, whose god is only what can be seen.

In contrast, the believer endures "as seeing him who is invisible" (Heb. 11:27). Christ Jesus frames everything in wisdom. Ecclesiastes touches the heart of things finally in chapter 12, verse 14 — "God will bring every work into judgment...whether it is good or whether it is evil." In other words, every action is valued by its relation to God and His purposes. Brief life has eternal worth. Whatever does not relate to Him is adrift and worthless. The world is God's gift to us, from heaven with love, wrought with exquisite consideration for maximum human contentment. It is part of the divine order of wisdom. Our worldly wisdom is only wise if it relates to the wisdom of the Creator. "Remember now your Creator in the days of your youth," says Ecclesiastes 12:1. "By wisdom the Lord laid the earth's foundations...The Lord brought [wisdom] forth as the first of his works, before his deeds of old...before the world began" (Prov. 3:19; 8:22-23, NIV). The creation of the world was an act of wisdom.

Edification Wisdom

This gift relating to the eternal business of God is not optional but indispensable for the building of the church. The church is not a secular and temporary organization but a creation of God planned from eternity (see Rev. 21 and 22). All that goes on in the church must be related to the purposes of God for redemption; then every gift will operate toward the same goal. Christ designed the present Christian age to be dominated by the Holy Spirit in world evangelism. The gift of the word of wisdom is God at the wheel keeping us headed in the right direction even when we are busy in matters which seem unimportant.

Paul said Corinthian believers "came behind in no gift" (1 Cor. 1:7, KJV). Nevertheless, they displayed an amazing aptitude for doing the wrong thing — even with the gifts. Their vocal displays of tongues, for example, were outside the framework of God's redemptive plan. They had nothing to do with edifying — upbuilding — the church. Gifts were treated as toys, not as power tools given to laborers by the Spirit. We are offered more than emotional satisfaction. We are wise master builders working according to the grace of God which is given unto us (1 Cor. 3:10).

"Wise master builder" is in Greek *sophos architechton*. An *architechton* is the word from which we get the English words *architect* and *technology* and so on, but it actually means a head builder. A *techton* is a craftsman in wood, metal or stone. Jesus was a *techton* (Mark 6:3) like Joseph (Matt. 13:55). God is called a "builder and maker" — *technites*. We get our word *technical* from the Greek *techne*, an art or craft; but our English *craftiness* is different, and the Greeks had a totally different word for it — *panourgia*, which stands for human wisdom. Paul speaks of this human wisdom in 1 Corinthians 3:19 as the opposite of divine wisdom.

A *technites* (craftsman builder) of the church needs *sophia* (wisdom). When the Lord ordered the making of the tabernacle in the wilderness, He said, "See, I have called Bezaleel...and I have filled him with the Spirit of God, in wisdom...and in all manner of workmanship" (Ex. 31:2-5). It was all "cunning" or intricate filigree, gold lacework. The direction of all God's works is toward the beautiful. And that applies to the church — any church — just as the tabernacle was enriched with golden furniture and brilliant tapestries. The robes of the high priest were for "glory and beauty" (Ex. 28:40). The church is the tabernacle of God (Rev. 21:3) to be adorned with wisdom, part of the beauty of Christ's bride.

What we have just said is from the same scriptures which Paul knew so well and which he expounds in 1 Corinthians 1 and 2. This fear-of-God wisdom given by God is what was in his mind when he spoke of the word of wisdom. It is not just a piece of good advice. It is a special word in season. The word of wisdom operates to bring us into proper relationship with God's eternal purposes. It overlaps with prophecy. Its center is the fear of the Lord, and it is therefore more than a wise consideration of all the facts and circumstances. It takes in all the facts we know and those which relate to God and, no doubt, facts to which the Lord alone has access, and places them in our minds as a principle or feel for what should be done.

Such a divine word comes to us for our everyday, practical circumstances, either personal or those of the church. It throws light upon situations and enables us to make right choices toward the unseen goals of God. "I understand more than the ancients, because I keep your precepts," said the young man, possibly a student-scribe, who wrote Psalm 119:100.

Wisdom's Secret Heart

Here is a mysterious revelation. Christ is the final meaning of wisdom. In him are "hidden all the treasures of wisdom and knowledge" (Col. 2:3). In 1 Corinthians 1:23-24 Christ is described as the wisdom of God, particularly "Christ crucified." If a word of wisdom is genuine it has a Calvary background, for Christ "became for us wisdom" (1 Cor. 1:30; see also Eph. 1:8,17). When we are pushed and pulled this way and that by stress, tempted perhaps by material or personal advantage, a word of wisdom will have the Calvary background with its reminder of other values.

James 3:15-17 declares that there is a wisdom which is "earthly, sensual, demonic" instead of that from above which is "pure, then peaceable, gentle, willing to yield, full of mercy." It was worldly wisdom which crucified Christ. A true word of wisdom enables us to take up the cross and discover the eternal dimensions of living by faith in God. That does not mean we shall be given a precise plan but that we will gain insight from the principle of action.

Wisdom, Not Bit and Bridle

A word of wisdom will be practical. This is not a gift of wisdom, but a word of wisdom. General wisdom is a quality available to us all, as James 1:5 says. The Lord has no intention of telling us when to sharpen our pencils or what to have to drink. Jesus never used bit and bridle to steer His disciples at every turn in the road. Freedom in Christ delivers His followers from a life under law, and God leaves large areas of our lives to our own choice and decision. Whatever we find to do in His name, He will bless.

Nevertheless, there are accounts in Scripture of directives coming from God. A word of wisdom may lead us to do something which normally would not occur to us. Samuel told Saul what he should do when looking for his father's donkeys. Instances of a word of wisdom are seen throughout the book of Acts. Paul warned the captain of a ship not to let the crew abandon the vessel (Acts 27:31-32). Ananias was sent to heal Saul and to give him insight into his future (Acts 9:10-19). James was given a wise word as the chairman of the important conference in Jerusalem when the relationship of Gentiles with the Jewish institutions was proving to be a difficult question (Acts 15:13-21). Paul had a word of wisdom directive to stay in Corinth because God had many people there (Acts 18:9-11).

I have heard very earnest preachers bringing people to make a vow at the altar to wait for God to speak each day. Many say, "I am waiting for a word of wisdom from the Lord." What they want actually is for God to make up their minds for them and relieve them of responsibilities. God does speak, and He spoke to men of old, but on no occasion did He speak when or because anybody was waiting for or asking Him to speak. God doesn't talk to order. The men and women God spoke to in Bible days were people getting on with whatever they had to do. No matter who tells us to do anything, we are personally responsible for what we do or don't do. Those who act only when they hear directions from God are living under law and not "the perfect law of liberty" (James 1:25). God wants us to grow up in Him, to be adults, not puppets moved by strings from heaven.

Believers are so often harried and anxious, looking over their shoulders wondering if they have done God's will, as if God quietly hid a blueprint every morning which was their first duty to find. This puts believers under a heavier burden than even the scribes imposed, for at least they could pinpoint a Scripture passage for what they thought God ordered. A wisdom greater than ours comes to us as free agents, not as a law of Sinai.

How the Gift Operates

A word of wisdom is not necessarily a dramatic pronouncement by someone standing up in a church. It may come in other ways. Maybe it will be during a conversation. Having wisdom from above, we consult with one another and talk, then a key is given to unlock the situation. It could come from anybody, even the least effective person present.

A word of wisdom may come by the Scriptures, the book of all wisdom. There is no doubt that it is the most common means that the Holy Spirit uses. Understanding frequently comes from hearing the Word to direct our footsteps. That is one reason why the ministry of the Word is so vital to us all. The Bible has the peculiar habit of speaking to us, even in the most unexpected way, in everyday situations.

Ministry which is experience-related or which offers specialized skills needs to be Word-related. Hundreds of seminars everywhere give advice for business matters and other areas of expertise for the work of God. Good as they may be, without the Word they will be inadequate. The wisdom of the business world should not be elevated above the wisdom of the Word and the word of wisdom, or being led of God. A word of wisdom is beyond human experience. It is revelation.

Wisdom may come through a chance remark or a casual comment. To the person speaking, it may seem like nothing, but it is propelled by the Spirit like an arrow, straight to the heart of a problem or need. It will be like all gifts "for the common good" (1 Cor. 12:7, NIV), enabling us to "walk in wisdom," especially to "those who are outside" (Col. 4:5).

Wisdom is described as treasure (Matt. 13:52; Rom. 11:33; Col. 2:3). The gift or manifestation is that treasure. It has a practical purpose. It may come in a manner which does not seem miraculous at all. God makes little fuss about anything. He works very quietly, almost secretly, and never tries to amaze us for the mere sake of amazement. It does not need to come in spectacular form. It is not just wondrous, but it touches the heart of a problem in a wondrous way.

A word of wisdom may come to us for ourselves, for somebody else or for a whole Christian group. For Paul it came personally, and for Saul it came through Samuel.

A word of caution about seeking a word of wisdom. One of the major purposes of this gift is to direct us. Some ask God to counsel them and show them in what way they should go. But how do they know He wishes them to go at all? It is dangerous to ask God to show you a new direction unless He has first given a word of wisdom indicating that He has a new direction for you. Perhaps He doesn't but wants you to carry on as you are. Then again, if He wants you to change direction, He would tell you anyway and not conceal it until you are in a mood to fast and pray to find out what it is. If He does not speak, it is because He has nothing to say and is satisfied with what we are doing. God is not a radio to be turned on at will. The Lord will let us know quickly enough if we are running in the wrong direction.

8

A WORD OF KNOWLEDGE

Millions of believers accept the gift of the word of knowledge as valid Christian experience. Usually it is understood as a revelation by the Holy Spirit of circumstances or details which would be spiritually helpful in the lives of individuals or churches.

For example, in the Birmingham Fire Conference in the United Kingdom in 1988 the Spirit told me the Christian name of a young man among the twenty-two thousand people present who was only there because he had been persuaded to come by his girl-friend. He was not really interested in the Christian life. I told the congregation, and the young man appeared on the platform where we prayed with him to receive Christ. Such incidents are not at all uncommon throughout the charismatic-Pentecostal world.

Yet we must begin with Scripture — not personal experience — and let that throw light on such matters. Let us begin with a saying from one of the wisdom books, Proverbs 30:24-25: "[Ants] are exceedingly wise." The trouble is that they have wisdom without knowledge. Ants are hardly walking encyclopedia. Humans, in contrast, are provided with vast amounts of knowledge, but like the wisdom tooth in our heads which is not greatly valued, moral wisdom also seems to have little place in the modern world. This is tragic considering that we have been printing the Bible for five hundred years.

If God gives a word of knowledge, it is unlikely to have trivial import or purpose. It will not be on the level of a crystal ball forecast that you will meet a tall, dark stranger. Knowledge itself in the Bible is not mere education, but something more important.

Right at the start we read, "You must not eat from the tree of the knowledge of good and evil" (see Gen. 2:17). Well, we know they did, and the first sin brought knowledge, but it was the knowledge of evil. It wasn't scientific knowledge either, but experiential. They knew pain, fear, guilt and shame. They also knew goodness, but only as a contrast to their wretched condition.

This is how it seems to continue. True science, beginning in the seventeenth century with Newton, Kepler and company, seemed like a shining dawn at first, but its horrific developments have brought the blood-red clouds of war and anguish. Knowledge fills our heads but not our hearts. A wiser race would have pursued some different course of knowledge.

We are concerned, however, with the divine knowledge. To be wise we have to know, and so the gift of a word of knowledge complements the gift of a word of wisdom. If a special word brings a particular circumstance to light, a word of wisdom may well be needed also to do what should be done. My collaborator, George Canty, had a word of knowledge during the night about a private meeting of his church elders; he knew all that had transpired. To know what to do the Lord also gave him a word of wisdom — "Show you know, but take no action." Following this course, the possible difficulties collapsed.

Whatever we find is meant by a word of knowledge, we cannot leave out of our study the fact that Scripture often talks of it and usually in a special sense. We know, in any case, that the Word of God remains the divine source of spiritual wisdom and knowledge. "Oh, the depth of the riches both of the wisdom and knowledge of God!" (Rom. 11:33). The written Word of God reveals the living Word, "in whom are hidden all the treasures of wisdom and knowledge" (Col. 2:3).

The manifestation gifts are too valuable to neglect: "Call out for insight and cry aloud for understanding...look for it as for silver and search for it as for hidden treasure...more precious than rubies" (Prov. 2:3-4; 8:11, NIV). Jesus describes knowledge as "treasure" (see Matt. 13:52). The alternative is, "My people are destroyed for lack of knowledge" (Hos. 4:6); they "withered away because [they] lacked moisture" (Luke 8:6).

The gifts are builder's tools for the edification of the church. God gives them because we need them.

One thing we must point out once again. In the New Testament the spiritual gifts are only for each local gathering of believers. There may be exceptional gifts which bring men from across the seas with an international ministry for exceptional circumstances, but the local church is intended to benefit from its own local gifts. This can be idealistic, depending on the size and state of the church, but nevertheless that is God's order of things.

What Knowledge?

The proper approach to our understanding of what is meant by a word of knowledge is to ask: What is this knowledge about? What does Paul mean by knowledge? He does not specify because he says so much about knowledge elsewhere. It is a favorite subject of his, the kind of knowledge extolled throughout Scripture — that is, not just academic Bible knowledge, but *understanding*. Psalm 119:100 speaks of knowing more than our teachers — that is, having a deeper feel for truth. Unbelievers have no knowing, because certain things come to us through the media of faith and love. To unbelievers, it is as foolish and hard to understand as microchip technology would have been to Queen Victoria. "The message they heard was of no value to them, because those who heard did not combine it with faith" (Heb. 4:2, NIV). Mental application will never make up for the absence of faith.

> At that time Jesus, full of joy through the Holy Spirit, said, "I praise you, Father, Lord of heaven and earth, because you have hidden these things from the wise and learned, and revealed them to little children...No one knows who the Son is except the Father, and no one knows who the Father is except the Son and those to whom the Son chooses to reveal him" (Luke 10:21-22, NIV).

In pursuit of our goal, here is a useful fact: the Gospel of John never uses the word *knowledge* but always *knowing*. To John, the true knowledge is not something memorized, as in a modern data bank. It is always something going on, dynamic, the participle *knowing*, not a static noun. It goes along with living, loving, seeing and believing. That puts us on the right track — true knowledge is going on knowing, like knowing a family member. A word of knowledge will relate to that.

Knowledge and Power

We pick up another clue from Matthew 22:29: "You are in error because you do not know the Scriptures or the power of God" (NIV). This would have staggered the rabbis. The scribes and others actually worked constantly on the Torah (the Law or Scripture). They knew much of it by heart and thereby expected to earn eternal life. What Jesus said about them was what they said about the common people whom they considered cursed for not knowing the Law.

He showed them the secret principle of knowledge: "If anyone wants to do His will, he shall know concerning the doctrine" (John 7:17). Today, many church leaders deny both the Scriptures and the power of God, something which even the Pharisees did not do. They treat the supernatural gifts as natural talents, tongues as linguistic ability, knowledge as education and wisdom as psychology (2 Cor. 3:14). Those who study a miracle book without belief in miracles are doomed to failure.

The Lamp That Never Flickers

The gift of a word of knowledge has a comprehensive sweep. It is what the Old Testament describes as understanding, insight of the heart. A computer has knowledge but no understanding. "Let not the wise man boast of his wisdom...but let him who boasts boast about this: that he understands and knows me...declares the Lord" (Jer. 9:23-24, NIV).

To Israel, God seemed to keep Himself at arm's length as the high and lofty One who inhabits eternity, known only through a third party — a prophet or priest. They only had information *about* God. In Jesus, God drew near in a manger, accessible, belonging to a family. The Son of God became the Son of man.

Then the knowledge of God became personal. Worship was no longer singing psalms to a transcendent deity on a celestial throne; it was given a new dynamic. He was one of us, our crucified, beloved Lord and Savior Jesus Christ. Christian worship began, Christ- and cross-centered. "The Lord of hosts" became "Abba, Father," the only name Jesus ever used about God. Here is knowledge, to know Him "whom to know is life eternal."

Opening up our knowledge of knowledge still further, we turn to Matthew 11:25-27. First, note that His Father was the "Lord of heaven and earth" but had revealed things to "little children" (NIV). In Luke 10:23 we are told He also said, "Blessed are the eyes which see the things you see." Note Christ's description of the Father — "the Lord of heaven and earth." He knew all that went on and could reveal it to whom He pleased.

There was special knowledge — the ultimate knowledge. "No one knows who the Son is except the Father, and no one knows who the Father is except the Son and those to whom the Son chooses to reveal him" (Luke 10:22, NIV). Jesus thanked the Father that certain things were hidden from "the wise and learned, and revealed...to little children" (Matt. 11:25, NIV).

The supreme knowledge was the knowledge of God. To know Him, however, is not all knowledge, which Paul says would enable us to understand all mysteries (1 Cor. 13:2). There is God's knowledge — as the Lord of heaven and earth — that includes "the secrets of...heart" which 1 Corinthians 14:25 says can be revealed through the prophetic gifts.

Now let us put all these clues together and see if we can define what knowledge is in a word of knowledge. These clues indicate quite a comprehensive knowledge. First, the basic knowledge, "to know God," which is only by revelation through His Son, our Lord Jesus Christ. The Bible calls it understanding, which means a living acquaintance with God. Second, a deeper heart-grasp of His

Word. Third, a divinely inspired sense of what is right and wrong or wise and foolish in life. Fourth, the Father knows all things, and they who know Him may have His confidence and share a little of what He sees.

This clarifies what we may expect from a word of knowledge. It is for us, to help us plot a wise course through life. The "Lord of heaven and earth" (Matt. 11:25) "works all things according to the counsel of His will" (Eph. 1:11). To know "Him with whom we have to do" (Heb. 4:13, KJV) is to walk surefooted in accordance with the direction of God's plans. We are all involved in His providences, like it or not. Without His showing us we shall blunder blindly and are in danger of being crushed by the irresistible movement of the predetermined will of God. We are thankful for the Word which is a lamp to our path, but many times we need a personal word of knowledge from God. It will come as a truth, a principle, an illuminating counsel, the highlighting of a passage of scripture or the spoken word of knowledge, or a combination of both.

The candle flame of human genius flickers briefly before being extinguished by the winds of time. The lamp of God never flickers. Jeremiah said, "O Lord, I know the way of man is not in himself; it is not in man who walks to direct his own steps" (Jer. 10:23). "It is God who...makes my way perfect" (Ps. 18:32). God possesses intimate knowledge of our lives even before we are born. "How precious also are Your thoughts to me, O God!...Such knowledge is too wonderful for me; it is high, I cannot attain it" (Ps. 139:17, 6). By the Word and a word of knowledge we can harmonize our ways with His eternal counsel.

Without instruction, the structure of our lives would collapse in chaos. This is exactly the state of those who have no knowledge of the Lord. Life for the unregenerate is meaningless confusion. As the famed librettist for the Gilbert and Sullivan operettas, Sir W.S.

Gilbert, is noted to have said, "Try we life-long, we can never straighten out life's tangled skein."

Knowledge and the Church

We have seen that knowledge involves the ways and purposes of God. One of His great activities is the church. That is certainly an area in which our lives must harmonize. In fact, the mystery of the church is the greatest divine project God has made known to us. That subject is what the gift chapters of Corinthians — indeed the whole epistle — are about. The gifts are for upbuilding the church. As we keep saying, if God gives them, we need them. They are not optional extras.

The gift of a word of knowledge is seen operating in biblical incidents in the careers of Joseph, Moses, Elisha, Daniel, Peter and others. Jesus had perfect knowledge about the woman of Samaria (John 4:16-19) and about Nathanael of Cana (John 1:47-49). Elisha knew the secret battle strategies of the king of Syria, or Aram (2 Kin. 6:8-23) — obvious instances of God-given communication. "The secret of the Lord is with those who fear him" (Ps. 25:14). "Surely the Sovereign Lord does nothing without revealing his plan to his servants the prophets" (Amos 3:7, NIV).

One afternoon in a hotel room I was praying, and the Holy Spirit began to speak to me. He impressed on my mind that a young man would come to the service that night whose name was John. The Lord gave me a message for him. I told the Lord that half the men in that city were called John, and if I just called his name it would sound ridiculous.

The Lord replied, "But his name is John!"

"Very well," I said, "I will obey You."

What I did not know, however, was that on the same morning a mother was praying for her son. The Holy Spirit told her, "Ask

John, your son, to come with you to the service, because I will call him out by name." Her boy was eighteen. She then begged him to come. Full of disbelief, he declared, "All right, Mum, I'll come. If God calls me out by name, my life will belong to Him."

In the evening service I gave the word the Holy Spirit had given me and called out for John. Not surprisingly, John was awed! This was a manifestation of the Spirit and the word of knowledge. He gave his life to Jesus that day. This account is true, and I still have the mother's letter on file.

We have spent the first part of this chapter showing that this gift is much more than prophetic flashes of knowledge about what is happening. The gift comes to people among people, not as a dark saying in secret. Having the knowledge of God is not for personal gratification or egotism, but for "the common good" (1 Cor. 12:7, NIV).

We can now make two statements: The Lord does not operate outside the Word. No revelation springs forth which runs counter to the Word.

Spurgeon is reputed to have said that there is no new truth, for if it is new it is not in the Word, and therefore not true. Even a word of knowledge or wisdom for a person or individual will directly or indirectly relate to Scripture.

A word of knowledge always aims at fellowship with God, even when it concerns the mundane. God may put in our minds what is in His mind about the world, and He seeks our cooperation.

Gifts in Practice

We often hear someone say, "I have a word from the Lord." That may indeed be so, but it does open up questions. First, what *are* these new utterances called "words from the Lord"? Are they words of wisdom, of knowledge, of prophecy, or what? Into what New Testament category do they fit?

Are they simply spiritual thoughts? They arise in all our minds if we follow the Lord. There is no harm in people rising in church to pass on something they have received or to interpret some picture that happens to float across their minds. If convenient, an opportunity might be given to approved members to minister in this way. But to dignify them with the authority of divine origin if they are little more than a passing thought is quite another thing. If we say we have a word from the Lord, it had better be one. If prophecy is to be judged, how much more a mere "word from the Lord"? Admittedly, many utterances don't need to be proved, since they would not mislead anybody. They are too slight, even though they may be given a majestic sound by phrases like "I, the Lord, do say unto thee."

With all we have learned so far about the gifts, we have to keep in mind that no prophetic utterance takes priority over the ministry of the Word of God itself. Prophecy must not displace preaching. People cannot live by "inspirationalism" but only by the bread of God, the Word.

If anyone disagrees and wants a church to become mainly prophetic, let him explain why that, in addition to these gifts and manifestations, God has given to the church apostles, teachers, pastors and evangelists "to prepare God's people for works of service, so that the body of Christ may be built up" (Eph. 4:12, NIV). Prophets do not usurp the place of apostles, pastors and teachers. The gifts of the Spirit are complementary to the Word.

Finally, there are two questions. First, how does a person know he or she has a word of knowledge? We shall look more closely at the mechanics of the prophetic gifts later, but we can note here that the promptings of God may be experienced in spirit, mind or body. Sometimes we may have no experience as such. We may speak a word of knowledge or of wisdom without realizing it, just as Caiaphas was said to prophesy without knowing it (John 11:49-

51). God may use a casual remark to somebody who needs it. During a conversation, one pastor laughed and said to another, "We know ever so many ways to do without the Holy Spirit." It affected the whole outlook of his friend.

Second, can this gift be taught? No. Nobody can learn a gift. But instruction can be useful. Teaching about gifts is necessary to recover a proper place for them in the church and to encourage reticent people who have held back the gift God has given them — in particular, speech gifts. Some need to value their gifts and understand how they operate. It is not impossible for those being taught a gift to receive the real thing, for it is received only by the Spirit. The Holy Spirit responds to seeking and willing souls. Otherwise, any learned technique remains what it is — a work of the flesh, not a manifestation of God's Spirit. Nobody can teach a manifestation, though we may all learn about it.

The Prophetic Ministry

Finally, we turn to some modern expressions and ask about their validity — phrases like "the prophetic church" and "the prophetic ministry." They are not unscriptural, and every ministry should be prophetic, but we wonder if it would be more biblical if we spoke of "the Word of God church," or "the Word ministry." That is always the conception of the church in the New Testament — "the pillar and ground of the truth" (1 Tim. 3:15). In Acts the expansion of the church is repeatedly described as "the Word of God grew and multiplied" (Acts 12:24). We have said that prophecy should not usurp teaching. When a church floats on prophecy, it needs to be anchored to the rock of the Word of God. Preach the Word!

Earlier we alluded briefly to a word of wisdom or knowledge coming via the exposition of the Word of God. The knowledge which Jesus Himself so highly valued and described as "treasure things new and old" is brought forth by the teacher or preacher of the Word (Matt. 13:52). It may not even seem supernatural, although the Word always is, even when it is not sensational. God often brings the critical word of knowledge to bear on our situation through what seems ordinary ministry.

The Word of God is active. The voice of the Spirit is often missed because the pulpit voice is listened to critically instead of with an open heart. To whom is God more likely to give a word of knowledge than the man waiting upon his ministry in the Word?

Knowledge and Public Ministry

Some men are announced as having a prophetic ministry, that is, they specialize in prophetic gifts, especially a word of knowledge. The following comments relate also to the whole question of the prophet and prophesying.

The word-of-knowledge type of career is something of a recent innovation, though being new does not mean it is to be rejected. The basic question is how prophets should operate, which comes down to a question of wisdom. It is simply a matter of method. For the rest of us, we must judge, hold fast to what is good and leave anything else alone.

Usually today, word-of-knowledge prophets bring a public emphasis to their work. The most frequent practice is to call individuals forward in front of a congregation to prophesy over them. There are no actual instances in the New Testament of this being done either occasionally or as the regular feature of anyone's ministry, just as other accepted church practices are also not found in the New Testament. The only criteria are the common matters of respect and wisdom.

There are assumptions we may question. Should a prophetic

ministry be announced or advertised? Must the Holy Spirit oblige every time? Can He be guaranteed to do what is expected of Him as advertised? The answer is, as we have seen, that there is no outright gift, but there are manifestations according to the will of God. No gift is an outright independent ability operating solely at will — like playing the piano — which could be announced beforehand.

There is another question many have asked. Should we expose individuals in a congregation to personal scrutiny either with or without the Spirit apart from the direct leading of God? Where there is a public mischief being perpetrated, a sin affecting the congregation — a sin of Achan, so to speak — then God may wish it to be exposed.

But if we are trusted with the secrets of human lives, is it for public knowledge? If God trusts us with a secret, should it not be for personal counsel to that individual alone? To inform an entire congregation that somebody's Christian marriage is breaking up or that a person has this or that weakness or even that they are good in some way brings nobody any benefit. It might give material for gossips or even leave someone in bad standing.

If a revelation ever describes a person's fault, then the Scriptures tell us what to do. "If a man is overtaken in any trespass, you who are spiritual restore such a one in a spirit of gentleness, considering yourself lest you also be tempted" (Gal. 6:1). We are not to tell the whole church. Nothing could be better guaranteed to do the devil's work than to accuse the brethren and so split a church. Christian procedures are strictly laid down both by Christ and by apostolic command. Love covers a multitude of sins. The real purpose of such a personal revelation would be, as 1 John 5:16 says, to pray about their sin, or, as Galatians 6:2 exhorts us, to "bear one another's burdens."

Another question arises: Does the expression *prophetic ministry* only belong to those who operate in a session of words of knowledge? Isn't a ministry of the Word also a prophetic ministry since the Word itself is always prophetic? Great prophets have sometimes been great preachers.

If we know anything about human nature, a man expected to operate prophetically will feel under pressure not to fail, though in fact he can only do what the Spirit allows him to do. Balaam is one example in Scripture (there were others) of a prophet expected to operate according to plan. He found himself in serious difficulties.

The possibility is that in trying to live up to congregational expectations, a person may bring revelations that originate from the imagination rather than from the Spirit. We wish it were never so, but many have been disenchanted after exciting statements "from the Lord" — some on very prominent and noted occasions. But do not let this detract from the fact that God's servants do have revelations by the Spirit.

I do not want to pronounce judgment but only to put forth thoughts that perhaps need time and study to settle. Unfortunately, words of knowledge have been heard that are so personal and related to so little in the church or the Word, or even the work of God, that the whole experience has become dubbed with some justification as "charismatic fortune-telling." Yet, rightly operated, it could be invaluable.

Again, as to failed prophecies and failed words of knowledge, human fallibility will occur. That does not invalidate a ministry unless it becomes frequent. Only the Word of God is inerrant. Even Agabus, named in Scripture as a Christian prophet, was not completely accurate in his utterances. He said the Jews would bind Paul at Jerusalem and hand him over to the Gentiles (compare Acts 21:11 with Acts 23:31). They did neither of those things. Other prophets in Acts were likewise limited. To be mistaken is possible, but wild and total inaccuracies and great pronouncements made halfway across the world that have proven to be nonsense have brought the gift into disrepute as mere hot air and bring into question whether the people concerned are prophets or not.

We learned a few pages back that wisdom and knowledge are complementary. A word of knowledge sometimes needs to be complemented by at least a word of wisdom. It can be healthy when a church's spiritual condition is described in the Spirit, but those exercising that type of ministry should consider how Christ judged the seven churches of Asia in Revelation. He always included a positive note of spiritual counsel and wisdom.

Knowledge and the Third Party

Scripture has much to say about all prophetic matters, and here is another current issue — prophetic knowledge and a third party. In the Old Testament covenant order, a priest or prophet was the channel by which the will of God was made known. The mind of the Lord was made known through Urim and Thummim (Ex. 28:30) or brought to the ordinary people by the elite and anointed class. This covenant has passed away. The glory of the New Covenant is that everyone is a priest, everyone is anointed, and everyone has access to God for himself or herself to know His mind and will.

It may be that confirmation may come through a word of knowledge, but it is no more than that. Guidance is direct. God told Cornelius to send for Peter, but He told Peter also, or Peter would have had nothing to do with it. "The secret of the Lord is with those who fear Him" (Ps. 25:14).

No third party, no prophet, priest, pastor or even an apostle need stand between God and believers. Nobody has the right to lord it over other believers in the name of the Lord as if they had a private communication from God about other people. Certainly others may be shown what God's will is for us, as it was shown to the men in Antioch about Paul and Barnabas, but it is never without the Lord's showing us also, as He had shown Paul and Barnabas (Acts 13:1-2). What each of us does is our own choice, and responsibility does not rest on other people's shoulders.

For example, Paul always kept his own counsel with God whatever others said, instanced especially before he was arrested. They told him not only what would happen, which was more or less correct, but what he should do, which was their interpretation of their own prophecy — and incorrect. God gives us wisdom, not instruction for action. To do what we feel is right before God is our glorious privilege and standing in Christ of which no man must subtly rob us. We must be discerning. The gift of discernment is often needed in the operation of other gifts.

We shall look further into the prophetic gifts when we come to look at prophecy.

9

FAITH

Faith risks everything on God, but God never lets us down. I remember an occasion when we were putting up one of our big tents. The ground was soft, and if a heavy rainstorm were to come, every fastening would have been pulled out. Then I saw that a rainstorm was on the way. To me it contained the leering face of the devil.

I stood and rebuked him and the black clouds moving toward us. If the tent collapsed, it would be dangerous for the vast crowd which would be inside, but I said to the men, "Go ahead. I shall preach in it tonight." I spoke with assurance in my heart, the faith of God. I said aloud to the devil, "If you destroy this tent, I shall get a bigger one." (I got a bigger one in any case!) I raised my voice and ordered that storm to leave us alone and then watched it divide, passing to the north and the south of our tent area. The ground remained dry and safe.

Faith is the pivot of our relationship with God. The whole Bible illustrates this. Nevertheless, no subject calls for explanation from the Scriptures more than faith and the gift of faith. We particularly want to bring help on this matter.

What Jesus said about faith is usually the first thing people quote: that with enough faith we could move a mountain (see Matt. 17:20; 21:21). But nobody has ever done it. No doubt many have experimented — usually with no great hope of success and perhaps with no idea of where to move a mountain.

No apostle did it, nor did Jesus Himself. God planned the landscape at creation, and I don't think He would want us shuffling the scenery about. The most frequent illustrations of faith in the New Testament are healings, but that need not be taken as the major use of the gift of faith. Why then did Jesus talk of moving mountains by faith?

For those wanting to reach a Bible understanding, here is something very important. Always read a whole passage and never just one verse. Don't tear texts out of the context of Scripture, such as this text about moving mountains. Matthew 17:20 concerns prayer against demons, and Matthew 21:21 relates to opposition and enemies. Mountain moving has to be understood in these contexts.

Now, about doing the impossible. Awful mistakes·have been made. To get to the heart of the matter we will enter the garden of Gethsemane with humble awe. The Son of God is praying about what is possible, and what He says penetrates to the very heart of the matter. Jesus said, "If it is possible, let this cup pass from Me; nevertheless, not as I will, but as You will" (Matt. 26:39). We must understand that only what is God's will is possible. A disciple who heard Jesus in the garden later wrote, "If we ask anything according to His will, He hears us" (1 John 5:14). Christ's prayer shows that what is *possible* is limited by the very evils Jesus came to overcome. It was not possible, for example, for God to save us from evil and also save His Son. Our fight against evil often presents a similar situation. To be what God sends us to be as His children witnessing in an alien world means that we are faced by evils.

Four times recently our evangelism campaigns have been cancelled. We were going to confront evils, but those evils were what brought about the withdrawal of visas and permits. God's will was not done. That is why we must pray, "Your will be done on earth as it is in heaven" (Matt. 6:10). Our lives have been under serious threat, but that danger could only be removed when the gospel entered the lives of our opponents. What is possible in such circumstances? It creates a dilemma, and we have to let God solve it. It is part of the process or fight against the devil. I said elsewhere that suffering and the ministry of healing seem inseparable. Nevertheless, mountains will be removed as we go on working and believing.

From Faith to Faith

At least four forms of faith are mentioned in Scripture:

- God has dealt to each one a measure of faith (Rom. 12:3).
- You have been saved through faith...the gift of God (Eph. 2:8).
- The fruit of the Spirit is faith (Gal. 5:22). The disciples asked of the Lord, "Increase our faith" (Luke 17:5).
- There is given to another faith by the same Spirit (1 Cor. 12:9).

We can describe these four kinds as follows:

- Common faith, which all men have
- Saving faith
- Faith, the fruit of the Spirit (ever-increasing faith)
- Faith which is the gift *(pneumatica charisma)*

This may oversimplify matters for the scholarly, but our analysis will help us to grasp what we mean by the gift of faith.

The Paradox

Many books are on the market to exemplify and build up faith. Nevertheless, the greatest is the Bible — the book of faith. It is the handbook showing us how faith operates, and it also gives us the faith we need to operate. "Faith comes by hearing, and hearing by the word of God" (Rom. 10:17).

Now comes the paradox. We also read that "[The Word] was of no value to them, because those who heard did not combine it with faith" (Heb. 4:2, NIV). We need faith to read the Word, but we need the Word to get faith. However, that little problem is not impossible to solve. Faith flows into the hearts of any who are open to it. Let the cynic remain a cynic, but the spiritual law is that faith brings faith — "from faith to faith" (Rom. 1:17).

Jesus explained this principle in Matthew 13:12: "Whosoever has, to him more will be given, and he will have abundance; but whoever does not have, even what he has will be taken away from him." The spirit of unbelief sours the soil and kills the seed of the Word.

We can take that a step further. Although faith is a gift, we are responsible if we do not possess it. It rests with us to believe or not to believe. It is our choice. Unbelief is not intellectual but emotional, an attitude of the heart. Nothing can possibly disprove God or show that to trust Him is wrong, but "not all have faith" (2 Thess. 3:2). That is, they have willed themselves not to believe, and they are "unreasonable and wicked" (2 Thess. 3:2) because they can believe, for God has "dealt to each one a measure of faith" (Rom. 12:3). It is a test of character, not of reasoning ability. Unbelief is sin, which is why "he who does not believe is condemned already" (John 3:18). Faith saves sinners although the nature of sinners is to rebel against faith. "Have faith!" Jesus commanded, and He commended those who do.

Faith is from God; it is His gift to us at birth, like sight or hearing. It is a faculty or a hand by which we reach out and accept what God has for us. If we destroy the faculty, or let that hand wither, then we can accept nothing. We are guilty losers.

The world conditions us. We go out in the morning, work all day, come in at night, read the newspaper, watch television; in all that time what have we been exposed to that will encourage faith in God? Usually nothing whatsoever — not a single thing. On the contrary, we have been virtually immersed in a sea of doubt and sin. The world is a vast, brainwashing establishment inclined to destroy faith in God. It maims us spiritually and amputates our hand of faith. We are "civilized" out of the simple nature God gave us.

A word of warning here. Faith is not a subject, like gardening or photography, just for those who are interested. We either believe or perish. Faith is a universal human obligation and responsibility. This is set out in the parable of the wedding feast in Matthew 22:12. All guests were provided with a wedding garment, meaning faith in the cleansing blood of Jesus. One man came, apparently thinking he could dress better than anybody else, wearing his own, possibly self-made, clothes. He was thrown out.

The standard dress in the kingdom of God is faith. "Without

faith it is impossible to please [God]" (Heb. 11:6). This one individual had come in, proud and superior, not wearing the garments of God-given faith. The kingdom of God is not based on academic achievements or merit. Entry permits, visas and passports are issued to the believing alone. Academic qualifications are irrelevant. Heaven will not be monopolized by theological graduates or by people who have "never robbed a bank," but only by people displaying the simple badge of faith.

Increasing Faith

Whatever form of faith we have — natural faith, saving faith, faith as a fruit or as a gift — its childlike quality remains. Believing isn't clever. Faith moves the mountains which doubt creates. It isn't the product of brilliance of thought, but of "looking unto Jesus, the author and finisher of our faith" (Heb. 12:2). We receive "the faith of our Lord Jesus Christ," as James 2:1 says.

What is faith? It cannot be quantified. There's no half-faith, 90-percent faith or anything like that. The poet Wordsworth described it as a "passionate intuition," "persuasion and belief ripened into faith."[1] That is what Jesus meant when He said, "If you have faith as a mustard seed" (Matt. 17:20) it could move mountains. Nevertheless we read about the "proportion of faith" (Rom. 12:6, KJV) — that is, proportionate to the demand made upon it. Jesus talked about little faith and great faith and asked, "How is it that you have no faith?" (Mark 4:40). Having no faith was the only thing that ever surprised Jesus (see Matt. 8:10). The vital thing to realize is that we can increase in faith. One form of that increase comes with the faith gift.

All increase of faith, such as the disciples asked for in Luke 17:5, is given by the Holy Spirit through the Word of God. It is impossible for faith to grow by prayer or worship alone. We may pray for faith, but we must also take the proper steps for our prayer to be answered, namely hearing or reading the Word. The less our understanding of the Word, the less our faith. We can have so little of the Word under our feet that we don't stand on faith but only balance on one toe. We may as well try to grow an apple tree on a damp cloth as cultivate faith from a paperback book of somebody else's experience.

The teaching of the Word is the only true way. This way a church can be strong, and its members can avoid doubts and not fall under the displeasure of the Lord. "Without faith it is impossible to please [God]" (Heb. 11:6). It is the only means by which there can be any genuine manifestation of the Spirit. Hearing about people's wonderful answers to prayer, healings or experiences is necessary and good, for God commands us to tell and testify; but often our doubts tell us that other people's miracles were only for them and not for us. They do not really create the kind of faith Christ wants. We see that in John 2:23-24, where faith based on miracles is shown to be inadequate. It is only faith in miracles, not faith in God. When miracles don't happen, faith can evaporate.

The Gospels more than once record that Jesus called people by the name of "little faith" *(oligopistoi)* (Matt. 6:30). We are what our faith is. It sums us up and determines our stature in God's eyes. Class distinctions are not recognized in the kingdom of God. Believers are the aristocrats of heaven. There is one class only: the faith people. Faith is the Christian's coat of arms and verification of spiritual nobility. Paul said God has not chosen "many noble" (1 Cor. 1:26), and James says He has chosen people to be "rich in faith and heirs of the kingdom which He promised to those who love Him" (James 2:5).

There was once an unknown and unnamed woman, not all that wealthy. She perceived that Elisha was a man of God. Unbelief would have been blind to it. She made a room for Elisha and gave him hospitality. The Bible calls her a "notable woman" (2 Kin. 4:8). She did not wish to be mentioned to the king or the army chief, for she was self-assured and made self-sufficient by her faith; in that lay her greatness. She is mentioned in the Hebrews 11 roll of honor, "and by it she obtained a good testimony" (Heb. 11:2). People of faith care little for those to whom the world gives its fading honors, as Jesus said, "How can you believe, who receive honor from one another?" (John 5:44).

Faith Defined

Unfortunately, faith has become a religious abstraction. All faith words in Scripture come from a root which connotes faithfulness, reliability in relationships and acting on the trustworthiness and honesty of somebody else. Faith is accepting the credibility of God — "He who promised is faithful" (Heb. 10:23).

Make a note of this — true faith is not in things happening,but is personal confidence in God. Faith means we leave things to Him and step out in trust.

The central Bible maxim is "Put your trust in the Lord," and that should be followed by the attitude "though He slay me, yet will I trust Him" (Job 13:15). Jesus expected that kind of trust when He made that most remarkable and paradoxical statement, "They will put some of you to death. All men will hate you because of me. But not a hair of your head will perish" (Luke 21:16-18, NIV).

Here are some valuable pointers to true faith:

- Faith is not merely being orthodox or being positive about doctrine, for we can be ultra-correct without any scrap of real trust in God.

- To try to bargain with God and say, "I will believe in You, God, if You answer this prayer," is gross ignorance of the whole matter. That is not trust.
- God doesn't always do what we think He should do; in fact, that is why we have to trust Him. If He always answered every prayer, faith would not be needed.
- We ask why, but who are we to demand to know why God does or does not do something as a condition for our trust? What sort of trust is that? It is so conditional that it fails to be faith altogether.
- God accepts no terms for trust. Must God conform to the reasonings of our puny minds to avoid being disbelieved?
- If we don't believe, it is our loss, not His.
- Faith cannot be measured; only the task undertaken in faith can be.

So far this chapter has dealt with faith in general. This has been absolutely necessary to clear the ground to talk about greater faith, or the gift of faith. The acquisition of faith is a major biblical topic. Its teaching applies as much to the gift of faith as any other form. Hebrews 11 lists the "elders" who obtained a good report all through one thing — faith. It calls them our witnesses or spectators as we run the faith race.

The Gift of Faith Defined

All faith is a gift, the work of God (John 6:29). Paul alludes to what Jesus said about faith moving mountains and links it with the gift of the Spirit in 1 Corinthians 13:2: "Though I have all faith, so that I could remove mountains." Earlier we said that not even Jesus moved mountains by the power of faith, but we do read, "By faith we understand that the universe was formed at God's command, so that what is seen was not made out of what was visible" (Heb. 11:3, NIV). Faith is the invisible reality.

That kind of faith power is treated as extraordinary in Scripture. The gift is a manifestation of the Spirit, as we saw, and this kind of faith has all the marks of the supernatural might of God. That is the gift. Faith is given by an act of the Spirit. It is useless to exhort congregations to exercise faith on that level. They can't have mountain-moving faith just by trying, like the old Welsh lady who tried to move the mountain that blocked the view from her window. She got up the next morning, saw it was still there and commented, "I thought as much!" Faith is not the product of striving, straining and concentrating. It is rest, not labor.

I preached in the Entertainment Center of Perth, Australia, which was packed with eight thousand people waiting to see a miracle. In faith, I said they would see one. I sat down on the platform and prayed, "Lord, where is the key miracle tonight?" The Holy Spirit whispered in my soul, "Look left — that lady in the wheelchair will be healed tonight." An assurance warmed me; she would be healed — that was the gift of faith.

When I stood up, I told the people what the Holy Spirit had put in my heart. I turned to the lady herself and with everyone listening asked her, "Madam, do you believe?" She was frightened and buried her head in her arms. In my heart I conferred with the Lord, saying to Him, "Lord, this woman doesn't even believe it." The Lord replied, "It doesn't matter. Today it is not her faith, but your faith that counts." "Thank You, Lord!" I answered.

By now the national television crew had arrived. I preached the message of salvation and then said to the audience, "Now the moment has come. I will go and pray for that lady to be healed." I walked to her and began to pray. Then I said, "Rise, in the name of Jesus." The woman looked at me as if I were crazy. Walk? Impossible! She attempted to stand but was very unstable. But I believed

God and encouraged her. "In the name of Jesus, walk!" Suddenly, the power of God shot through her very bones. She jumped forward and then ran, while eight thousand people roared in praise and wonder to God. The TV team caught the whole episode on camera.

This lady had suffered from brittleness of bones and was not expected ever to walk normally again. But what is impossible with men is possible with God. I met her two years later, still perfectly healed. What is of faith lasts forever.

The Gift of Faith in the Local Church

Viewing the exploits of men and women like Moses and Elijah, or George Müller and Smith Wigglesworth, we may feel very small. Yet they in themselves were not special. Elijah "was a man subject to like passions as we are" (*homoiopathes* — "same feeling") (James 5:17, KJV). They were simply raised up in their times for enterprises which obviously called for the courageous faith gift which God granted them. Their boldness in God challenged the world.

We now come to the heart of the question. What is the gift of faith? So far as is practical, we will start with a definition. The gift of faith is the manifestation of the Spirit imparting a special faith needed for a special work which God puts before us. The work may be large or small, but faith is a gift to everyone who needs it in order to do whatever they should do.

The illustrious names of certain nation-moving and world-shaking people of faith are constantly given to us. But why just these? Are they really the privileged few? The truth is that whoever does the will of God, whether in a sphere large or limited, will enjoy this same resource. If tongues and prophecy are available to us in our town or village church, why are we afflicted with a sense of inferiority that supposes other gifts are only for eminent leaders? If one gift, then all gifts are available according to God's will.

Where the Church Is

All gifts, including the manifestation of faith, are for the local church. The Corinthian church, Paul testified, came "behind in no gift" (1 Cor. 1:7, KJV). True, nobody in Corinth ever moved mountains or by faith plucked up trees and planted them in the sea, but the gift of faith was theirs according to their opportunities and local problems. Spiritual gifts are not the exclusive equipment of world leaders or those prominent in what we call the "wider church."

At this point we shall have to make a digression. The word *church* simply means a gathering or congregation *(ekklesia)* and is so used both in Old and New Testament Greek. It does not signify an organized official membership, for such a thing was unknown in the New Testament.

Early on there were sometimes many churches or congregations in houses in one city. If they all came together, then that also would be called the church; that is, a gathering. We speak of "the Anglican church," but each local congregation in a service is the church. The Methodist church is the name given to Methodists worldwide, which is a convenient term, but the actual *ekklesia* is wherever born-again Methodists meet.

There is nothing whatsoever in Scripture obliging all Christians in a city to belong to one church. It speaks of the church in Ephesus or Philippi, but there are not even the flimsiest grounds to teach that we can only have one church in a town, village or area like Hackney or Brooklyn. If we want to do it that way, that is up to us. God doesn't interfere with what we organize. He gives us the wisdom to arrange our Christian fellowship with practical convenience, whether independent or denominational. The pattern was still developing when the New Testament was written.

God blesses us in all kinds of situations. When our gospel crusades are backed by all the Christian churches in a city, those congregations are the church. One day when all believers are caught up to be with Christ forever, then that gathering to Christ will reveal the universal church, all one in Christ.

Gifts for the Local Church

Now that digression about the church was important. It tells us where the gifts of the Spirit may be manifested. When we read of the five-fold ministry of men whom Christ gives to the church, it is widely assumed that they are for the world church or for a whole group of churches. But no such universal church or group of churches existed when Paul was writing. When he speaks of gifts for the church, it is Christ's ideal for each individual assembly (Eph. 4:11), though the ideal is not always reached.

That is the Word of God, however much we may have to adjust our traditional thinking. The aim is to build people up to the full stature locally, blessed with all spiritual blessings and all gifts as was the Corinthian church. While the church is simply a gathering, it is also a gathering of faithful and regular people. All the pastoral epistles assume that there are a number of recognized members who constantly meet, forming a stable assembly. Wanderers from church to church claiming they are members of the world church would be under suspicion in Paul's churches, as no church could be built at all if everybody was so fickle. Each assembly is recognized by God as a spiritual entity in its own right and qualifies for the gifts whether or not it has links to other churches.

According to the Task

According to our call and sphere of service, God gives us faith. We have faith for every task, whatever God wants us to undertake. We don't read that Smith Wigglesworth parted the sea like Moses or that Moses healed the sick like Wigglesworth. We don't read that Müller brought down fire from heaven or challenged the monarch on his throne like Elijah, but Elijah did not feed two thousand orphans by faith. Each according to his place.

If mountains must be moved, there will be faith to do it and not until then. There are leaders exercising ministries literally affecting nations. They are doing just what they are called to do — and they exercise faith for that. Not all see mighty healings; that is not their gift, but they take evangelism into all the world. Their faith gift is conspicuous. Nevertheless, when we labor out of sight in some remote corner of the world, the same gift will operate.

Faith and Obedience

The faith gift makes all things possible. Even ordinary faith produces outstanding people, though not all church members are notable examples of its galvanizing power. Some are still at the growth stage where they declare that they would go through fire and water for God — but only if it doesn't rain. Paul and Silas in Philippi, sick with horribly mutilated backs, had a celebration meeting in the pitch-dark prison and then conducted a baptismal service before they had recovered from their terrible mauling. That is not all, for we read that when they left, "they [Paul and Silas] encouraged them" (Acts 16:40). Paul and Silas, battered and wounded, comforted the brethren they left there.

That is the kind of possibility which the gift of faith opens up. This is rather different from the practice of staying away from worship on Sunday in case the cold caught in the rain at the football game on Saturday gets worse, or to catch up with work that we didn't do during the week when we were watching "interesting" nonsense on television, or because we feel tired. The Lord says, "Those who honor Me I will honor" (1 Sam. 2:30). Believe it, and our habits will change — and our health!

Now we can learn something from the two words *faith* and *obedience*. The Greek words for unbelief, *apistia*, and disobedience, *apeitheo*, belong to the same root. To obey God you need faith, but faith is given when you obey. Obedience is faith, and faith means doing what God says. Not being able to do it is no excuse, for we can by faith. He offers us the resource of the gift of faith. Prodigies are possible. Ordinary people can expand their potential, and to that history is witness. Jesus challenged His hearers: "What do you do more than others?" (Matt. 5:47). If we are "faithed" by the Spirit, we can tackle the impossible.

That is the characteristic of Christianity. The hallmark of God's work in us is that He dispatches us into worlds nobody else has ever conquered. Study the story of Peter walking on the water in Matthew 14:22-33. Three miles out on the sea of Galilee the disciples saw Jesus gliding toward them on the water. They shrieked themselves hoarse with superstitious terror, thinking He was a ghost. Jesus called to them, "It is I" (v. 27).

Now Peter knew Jesus. He knew there was only one person in the universe who would do what Jesus would do — tell Peter to do the impossible. That was the acid test of His identity. Peter challenged the apparition, saying, "Lord, if it is You, command me to come to You on the water" (Matt. 14:28). Jesus did challenge him. Peter walked on the waves toward Christ. That was a manifestation of the gift of faith.

Jesus is the one who calls men and women to be greater than they think themselves to be. If you are thinking of following Jesus, you should know He is like that. He doesn't call you just to hold a lily or pick buttercups. The tongue-tied preach. Fishermen become fishers of men. Harlots become lovers of God. Handicapped people walk. That shows it is Jesus, the true God, who sends you to undertake what you would normally never consider.

Of course, doing what He commands also identifies the true believer and reveals the gift of faith. By my God I can run through enemy troops. "I can do all things through Christ who strengthens me" (Phil. 4:13). Nobody has faith to move mountains until mountains need to be moved. But there is faith to do whatever God bids us do — when we do it. The size of faith is not the right language. The necessary size of the tool of faith will be handed out to us according to the size of the job.

Formula Faith

To speak and make a positive "confession" in faith is obviously an excellent practice. Positive language helps positive attitudes.

We must not turn this into a doctrine, however, for it is not in the Bible. The secret of getting God to do things does not lie merely in saying the right thing, getting the formula right or speaking positively. It is alarming to suggest that God can be made to act if we only speak with the proper technique, as if saying something makes God do it. If it seemed so — and there are always testimonies to anything — then those concerned also had faith in their hearts, which was the actual cause. Faith activates the miraculous. That is the dynamic.

David's challenge to Goliath has been used as an example illustrating how victory comes through positive confession. What is not mentioned is that Goliath also spoke a positive confession — and lost! No amount of positive shouting will deceive God if we are not acting in obedience and trust in Him, and if we don't believe in our heart, as Jesus said.

There are ample Bible instances that do not fit this "miracle in your mouth" formula. David in fact confessed negatively — "I shall perish someday by the hand of Saul" — but he didn't, as you know!

However, our object is not merely to comment on formula faith, but to show that it is faith that operates, whatever shape it comes in. Those proclaiming their discoveries and innovations back them up with many testimonies. No doubt, but it is not the techniques and teachings which bring success; it is the underlying faith in God. God cannot be made to jump when we press the right button and say the right thing, but God does honor faith, even when it comes larded over with peculiar ideas. As articulate beings we must articulate our faith, but whatever the words in our mouths or the nonsense in our heads, God sees only what is in our hearts. As the great hymn says, "Faith, mighty faith, the promise claims and cries it shall be done."

10

HEALING, PART ONE

The gift of healing draws great interest, so we must give it very careful attention. It embraces so many different views, many of which are not scriptural. Some want to disprove it, and others have extreme views that say we need never be sick or even die. The subject is a minefield, but we will plot a course by the Word of God, first about healing in general and then about gifts of healings.

Why God Heals

Healing, as we shall explain it here, began with Jesus. There have always been superstitions, prayers to the gods, healing waters such as we read of in John 5, and so on, just as in the world today. Those bitten by snakes were healed as they believed and looked on the serpent of brass made by Moses (Num. 21:8-9), which Jesus Himself referred to in John 3:14. The healing ministry of Christ was totally new and startling, however, and for that matter so is the ministry of Christ today through His believing churches.

What Jesus did gives us some fundamental truths.

Jesus healed without any condition or pressure on people to be converted. Of course, He did seek the lost people of His day, as He does those of our day, but whether they believed He was the Son of God or not, He healed them. His compassion was unhesitating and universal. When a foreign soldier said his servant was sick, Jesus immediately said, "I will come and heal him" (see Matt. 8:5-13). His work among the sick was a demonstration of the truth of divine grace.

Jesus acted in the name of God the Father and so demonstrated the truth that health is the normal blessing of God, as the sun and rain are for the just and unjust. He healed without obligation for love, not for effect, because the sick were sick.

Christ did not love just for soul but for people. He had concern for their physical needs. God loves the world *(kosmos,* the inhabited globe) — all His creatures; not a sparrow falls from the housetop without the Father's knowing, Jesus said. By healing the afflicted, Jesus asserted that He was doing the Father's work and showing what God's attitude really is toward everything that breathes.

Yet Jesus' whole ministry was more than physical cures. He said in every way possible that the whole man needed help — physically, psychologically and spiritually. He wanted to do far more than heal, and He said that it was not useful for a man to be sound in body if he went into hellfire. He was disappointed when people went away too easily content. "You only come to me for bread that perishes, not for the bread of heaven that gives you everlasting life" (John 6:26-27, author's paraphrase), He sadly told them. He wanted them to read His wonders as signs, spelling out the tremendous truth of a vast heart of love that was beating for them. He wanted them to know that they needed God. Often people accepted the hand out of a cure but turned away and stayed outside the comprehensive benefits of the kingdom of God.

Jesus was not a mere social reformer. His method was intensely personal; He was concerned with the entire personality. The point of the healing of the woman with a hemorrhage in Matthew 9:18-22 was not so much the healing itself as it was His personal concern for her. Closely pressed by a peering crowd, He calmed her fears and assured her of salvation. She had taken healing touching from His robe, but He couldn't just let it go at that. He wanted it to be personal so everybody would know it was a love gift from Him to her.

Christ sought to create a relationship of praise, thankfulness and worship between the sick and His Father. After He had healed the blind man in John 9, Jesus found him and asked, "Do you believe in the Son of God?" (v. 35). The episode ends when the man says, "Lord, I believe" (v. 38). And he worshipped Him.

Jesus instructed the disciples to heal the sick and then, beyond that, they must proclaim the real good news, the gospel, that "the kingdom of God has come near to you" (Luke 10:9). He healed the leper (Mark 1:41-45) and sent him to offer a sacrifice of thanksgiving as a testimony. He healed ten lepers (Luke 17:12-19), but only one, a Samaritan, came back to thank Him. Jesus remarked, "Were there not ten cleansed? But where are the nine? Were there not any found who returned to give glory to God except this foreigner?" (vv. 17-18). He wanted those healed to have more, to establish a relationship of worship with God.

Even in the beginning, Moses said to Pharaoh, "This is what the

Lord, the God of Israel, says: 'Let my people go, so that they may hold a festival to me in the desert' " (Ex. 5:1, NIV). Pharaoh did not question it. Israel was released for God's praise in the earth, and their song of praise is recorded over and over throughout Scripture.

Jesus often gave people deliverance before they turned to God, even if they failed to turn to Him nine times out of ten — a fair average perhaps in our gospel meetings. Healing may be an end in itself if that is all we want. But from God's angle, it is to open our hearts to more love.

Here is an all-important summary to be learned well: To know and love God is more important than healing. Many go unhealed despite prayer and faith, but healing is not everything. Sickness is not the ultimate evil, nor are cures the ultimate good.

It is absurd to lose faith when healing does not come. God does far more than heal, and He does not fail. There are infinitely higher benefits for which Christ labored and died. In fact, healing only takes on meaning, significance and value when it opens a soul to the love of God. Then it becomes a sign which they have read.

Healers Who Suffer

There is a strange background to healing. "By His stripes we are healed" (Is. 53:5). That scripture we know well enough. But it has a neglected dimension. Those who go with Christ to heal will know something of His stripes. He sends out those who are ready to suffer. Jesus sent out His disciples to heal the sick and at the same time warned them that they were called upon to suffer and be persecuted (Matt. 10:7-42). Healing and cross-bearing go together. They may even suffer sickness, as Paul apparently did, as he told the Corinthians (see 2 Cor. 12:7). At least any firsthand experience generates sympathy with the afflicted. Healing and suffering are destined to go hand in hand. Somebody suffers, whoever is healed.

Perhaps you want a healing ministry? Then alongside the glory be prepared for tears, heartache, disappointment, frustration and persecution. The price for others' wholeness was Christ's brokenness. Those who minister His grace best will share something of Christ's inner heart.

Then there is the completely irrational attitude of the world. Those who pray for the sick will be attacked. The world will make those suffer who bring divine relief for suffering. There are men who write clever books against divine healing and who never lift a finger to bring any sufferer relief.

The Problem of the Unhealed

If you want the gift of healing, you will certainly come up against the question of suffering. What do you say when prayer for the sick seems unanswered? In fact, this question is bound up with what we have been saying: that Jesus heals because He suffered. I need to explain that. Remember that what Jesus was, He still is — "the same yesterday, today, and forever" (Heb. 13:8). What Jesus was on the cross, He is on the throne — the Lamb slain from the foundation of the earth. He never changes; He is the eternal God. God heals because He suffers.

If God suffers, what a world of truth that opens up! It is as if He takes the responsibility for all the evil in the world. He accepts it into His own infinite experience. He carries our sorrows. He cares for us. He absorbed the tragedy of the fall into His own being. He took the shrieking discords of sin and misery and wrote them into the score of the eternal symphony of love — the everlasting sounds of heaven, the eternal music of His being. But that same truth gives us the most powerful hope of His healing. Wherever He wills, He relieves the oppressed and delivers the afflicted.

However, no Christian should sit and fatalistically accept sickness, either his own or anybody else's, as the mysterious will of God. Our God is not mysterious when it comes to healing. We wage war against sickness, since it is a mark of evil. Though we cannot make a wholesale end of it and cure everybody in sight at present, that is no reason why anybody should not be healed.

Healings Belong to the Kingdom

Next, there is an issue upon which we must make the most careful distinction. Miracles do authenticate the gospel, but that is not the reason for miracles. In fact, it is a gross error to suppose that God heals the sick just to prove something or establish something. If that was the object, then lack of healing would have the opposite effect and disprove Christianity. But, in fact, when the sick stay sick, it disproves nothing.

One form of this error comes from the school of thought that says healings were only a temporary gift — given at the beginning of the Christian faith in order to establish it. It really is a shocking and scandalous suggestion. Is God like that? Healing the sick not for their sakes, but for His private interests? Did God really use afflicted people just as a convenient opportunity to work a few miracles until Christianity was set and then show no practical interest in them any longer? Is that love — or heartlessness?

We have said elsewhere that Paul's reference to the *charismata* in 1 Corinthians 12 is part of his doctrine of the church; that is, the gifts are a basic feature of the church. Nowhere is there the slightest suggestion that what was built into the church has now been taken out.

It was certainly part of the original truth. They preached a Christ who healed, and that is how the evangelists proclaimed Him in Matthew, Mark, Luke and John. What right has anybody to preach a Christ who does not heal if they preach the Christ of the four Gospels?

If God did not intend this mercy to be extended to our times, we certainly don't get that impression by reading Scripture. At least there is no statement that makes that at all clear. On the contrary, every statement assumes Christ never changes, that He continues the work He began.

Jesus sent the disciples to proclaim the kingdom of God. Miracles of healing were the proof of the power of that kingdom. Where is the kingdom without that evidence? For centuries the church lacked such genuine power signs. Instead it transferred the whole idea of the kingdom into the temporal authority of the church, turning the kingdom into an empire which dominated kings and kingdoms through the pope of Rome. This followed Augustine's book *The City of God.*

If we deny miracles — as many did and still do, whether liberals or even evangelicals — we change the character of the gospel we preach. A nonmiracle gospel is reduced to a purely spiritual religion, ineffective on earth. If we do that, then somehow we are left with the necessity of making such a heavenly teaching relevant, for it pretty well ceases to be so for people walking around in shoes on earth. The real gospel needs nobody to show it to be relevant — it just is. The baker never yet had to argue that his shop is "relevant." The gospel is the bread of life, bringing life and healing to mind, body and soul — preach it, and all the world sees it matters.

The kingdom of God has been introduced on earth, and healing shows it. Unless it continues that way, how do we know it is the same gospel? The gospel witnesses to itself by signs following. Without healing it is stripped of a powerful element of its own authentication. Healing is not detachable, a mere bit of gadgetry or an accessory. It is integral to the gospel.

Do we really preach Christ? Yes! Then Matthew shows that wherever Jesus went, when He moved from one place to another, He always healed. It was a consistent habit of Christ. Peter also said that healing is what He went about doing. That is Jesus!

The Gift

Now we come to the gifts of healings. The expression *gift of healing* is not mentioned in the Bible. It is a useful term, but unfortunately it has been appropriated by spiritualist healers, psychics, New Agers and others. However, Christians were practicing healing long before the modern healing epidemic (as somebody called it) began.

Paul always uses the plural expression, "gifts of healings." It occurs three times, in 1 Corinthians 12:9,28,30. These plural gifts are from one person to another; that is, many healings through one individual acting as a steward for healings to be given to the needy and afflicted. If we put the context of this gift together with it we would read, "To another is given the manifestation of the gifts of healings," or in more common terms, "the gift of the gifts of healings." This is not a commission to heal everybody, but only those for whom the Holy Spirit gives a manifestation.

Healing Words

Let's look carefully at the word for healing that is originally found in the Bible. In 1 Corinthians 12:9 it is "physical cures" *(iama/iaomai)*. It is not used for anything else, except metaphorically a few times. This is the ordinary word for medical recoveries. Luke, the beloved physician, uses it most often: thirteen times.

Two other words used for healing are the Greek *sozo* and *diasozo*, which occur ninety-seven times and are translated "to heal" sixteen times. Its best equivalent in English is "to make whole," whether spiritually or physically, as in Mark 6:56: "As many as touched him were made whole" (KJV). *Sozo* was used by Greeks writing to their friends, especially in parting as a wish for good health.

144

It is a fundamental fact that as human beings we are not only flesh, but spirit. The two are inextricably joined, and to distinguish what is of the body and what is of the spirit is often impossible. The Bible teaching on this bond is not a side issue but is at the core of scriptural revelation, including the whole issue of salvation. Any theology which tries to divide the benefits of salvation between body and soul is bound to be artificial.

That is how early Christian fathers viewed it. Irenaeus, the disciple of Polycarp who knew the apostle John, declared in *Against the Heresies*, "The body is capable of salvation." Justin Martyr, who died in A.D. 165, also declared that God saves man, not part of a man; not his soul alone, but the body also.

Another term is used in Mark 16:18: "They will lay hands on the sick, and they will recover." The phrase "will recover" here is literally "get well" *(kalos exousin)*, a process of recuperation.

Four different words are used in Luke 17:11-19 for the healing of the ten lepers: mercy, cleansing, cure and healing *(eleeson,* have pity; *ekatharistesan,* was cleaned; *iasthe,* was cured; *sesoken,* has healed). These are also salvation words, but they are certainly used for physical deliverance here.

The most frequent term for *healing* in the New Testament is "therapy" *(therapeia, therapeuo),* occurring forty-five times. It relates to the process or means of cure.

It has been said that there are no gradual cures in the New Testament. In fact, not one of the Greek words quoted above suggests instant recovery. For example, a gradual work is indicated in the case of the ten lepers. They were healed "as they went." They were going from Galilee to Jerusalem, which would take two or three days. What we know of any Old Testament cures is that they were gradual recoveries. We know some cures were immediate, but only because we are explicitly told this. In Mark's Gospel, *immediately* is a favorite expression for other action besides healing. Peter was an immediate sort of man and is thought to be behind Mark's Gospel. Immediate healing impressed him. Instant recoveries are far more memorable. That is also the case today.

The Old Testament has no equivalent Hebrew word for the English *health*. Not to be ill was taken as the natural state. Sickness was considered to be a withdrawal of natural life by God. This stems from Genesis 2:17: "You must not eat from the tree of the knowledge of good and evil, for when you eat of it you will surely die" (NIV).

Sin brought about loss of vitality and the beginning of death. All recovery was taken as forgiveness. The restored favor of God restored the life-energy from God which normally sustained everybody, saving people from death. Diseases and plagues represented the curse of God. They exhausted human life-forces, leading to silence and inactivity in the grave, where praise to God ends.

That was the general teaching before Christ. Typical of this is Psalm 103:1-4, "Praise the Lord, O my soul…who forgives all your sins and heals all your diseases, who redeems your life from the pit" (NIV). It goes on to contrast "the pit" with a return to youthful vigor, "Your youth is renewed like the eagle's" (v. 5, NIV). Healing and forgiveness are invariably spoken of together in the Old Testament. See Psalm 32:1-5 for a typical example.

In 2 Chronicles 16:12, King Asa turned to the doctors instead of seeking God. This has been grossly misunderstood. It is not a condemnation of doctors. It has been taken as the grounds for saying believers should not go to doctors. Scripture does not speak against medical doctors. The real explanation is that King Asa had sinned and believed that was why he was sick. Instead of repenting and seeking forgiveness first in order to be healed — as he very well knew he should — he asked the doctors to cure him, to outwit God as it were and to get him well without repentance or forgiveness.

More Light

In the New Testament, the Lord brings us far more light. He changes or qualifies the idea that if a person suffers, they must personally be guilty and deserving of judgment (though we all are). It was that idea which caused so much puzzlement to Job and his friends and to the writers of many psalms, such as Psalms 37 and 73. He still keeps before us the facts that sin and suffering are linked and that hell awaits sinners, but He also recognizes that the innocent suffer.

Jesus shows particular concern for the victims of other people's wickedness. The struggle of fathers and mothers, the distress of children, the bereaved, the frightened, the demon-driven, the unwanted and outcasts, the hungry, the untouchables, refugees and all those who had done nothing to deserve such miseries. The sick came to Him like an endless river. They touched His heart, and over them He shed tears and, finally, His blood. He championed the cause of all sufferers. To offend one of His little ones (we are all His little ones, incidentally), He said, would bring such woe upon the offenders' own heads that to be dropped in the sea with a millstone around their necks would be more pleasant.

To understand sickness, we have to learn that there is a universal disturbance of the order of God to which we all contribute. Personal sin makes us more vulnerable to the prevailing conditions of evil, so a sickness could well be linked to our own failure. In Christ's day the sad masses believed afflictions branded them as sinful. This added to their distress. Jesus showed them He was forgiving and caring. Guilt could be lifted from their consciences to give them the peace of heaven in their souls.

When He said, "I have come that they may have life" (John 10:10), they understood it better than many do today as meaning life for body and soul. He told a paralyzed man he was forgiven

(Matt. 9:2), and told the disciples, "Peace [*shalom*] I leave with you" (John 14:27); that is, well-being and prosperity. The congregation in the Nazareth synagogue (Luke 4) would clearly understand that healing was intended as Jesus spoke from Isaiah 61:1-2, especially when He used the specific illustration of the healing of Naaman the leper.

Sometimes mistaken theology produces mistaken translation of the Bible. One we ought to correct is John 9. Seeing a blind man, the disciples began to philosophize, asking who had sinned — his parents or himself — before he was born (as if he could!). Jesus said, "Neither!"

Wrong punctuation of verse 3 has disguised what Jesus did. For example, the New International Version says, "This happened so that the work of God might be displayed in his life." That surely amounts to libel upon God. Jesus used the imperative: "Let the work of God be done!" The Greek uses no causal term. It does not suggest that the man was born blind in order to be healed. Correctly this verse should read, "This man has not sinned, nor his parents, but let the work of God be done in him. I must work the work of God while I am in the world."

In other words, the work of God was not to make people blind, but to give them sight. God made eyes from clay at creation, and Jesus repeated the process for this blind man. "As long as it is day, [I] must do the work of him who sent me," Christ said (v. 4, NIV). Jesus was doing what the Father did, and added, "While I am in the world, I am the light of the world...For judgment I have come into this world, so that the blind will see" (vv. 5, 39, NIV). John 9 is put there to show that God does not inflict people or cure them just to make a point.

11

HEALING, PART TWO

Now we are ready to tackle the phrase gifts of *healings*; that is, multiple gifts for multiple sicknesses. Many guesses have been applied in interpreting this phrase, particularly that it means one person can heal one thing and another person heal something else; one the blind, another the deaf, and so on.

Some have interpreted the gift by their experiences — always an unsafe procedure. They have found one particular affliction being cured, or cured more than other troubles, and they have taken that to mean that they have "found their gift," as they say. One spoke of himself as an arthritis specialist. Leg-lengthening plus the claim of a discernment to detect sufferers from a short limb is another specialist's healing claim. God does adjust limbs, of course, but this "gift" is open to question. Measuring a leg is notoriously difficult, even for hospitals. An imperceptible movement of the hip, made even involuntarily, can produce the impression of a limb growing. This kind of healing looks suspiciously like a technique rather than a miracle. Onlookers sometimes wonder whose leg is being pulled!

In Scripture, nobody specialized in one affliction. Like salvation, healing is to the "whosoever." A single-affliction gift — for deafness say, but not for heart trouble — would be discrimination. An evangelist would never offer God's forgiveness for theft, but not for adultery. Our faith should rest on God, not on healing; it should not be limited to what we have seen God heal. If we only see one sickness cured, and only believe for that, it is all we will ever see.

It is time to get back to the Word. Jesus healed "every disease and sickness among the people" (Matt. 4:23, NIV); Peter did also. People brought to him their "sick and those tormented by evil spirits, and all of them were healed" (Acts 5:16, NIV). By the apostles' hands "many signs and wonders were done among the people" (Acts 5:12). We that when Paul was on the Isle of Malta, "the rest of the sick on the island came and were cured" (Acts 28:9, NIV). A gift of healing for only one specific affliction has no Bible precedent.

Building Up Hopes?

If you pray for the sick you will find accusations being made that you are heartless, building up hopes and sending some home unhealed. Following my Fire Conference in Frankfurt, some German clergy were reported in the press as making this kind of allegation. The fact that countless people were healed apparently should not have happened in case others were not healed! It is hard to understand the kind of mentality which supposes that it is a higher virtue to heal nobody than to heal only a few hundred. I know many German clergy who practice on this high moral ground, showing compassion on the sick by not praying for any of them! I am sure they disappoint one person — the Lord Jesus Christ Himself.

One woman was carried onto the Frankfurt platform with a few days to live. She was dying with cancer. In front of eight thousand people, God gave me the key miracle He promised and raised her up. If her cure cost others dashed hopes (which is not true), we must leave that to God.

If anybody thinks we ought not to build up people's hopes in case they are not healed, they had better advise the afflicted never to open their Bibles. The Word of God is without doubt the worst offender in building up expectations! In fact, I, like most of my colleagues, would never have laid hands on anybody without Bible authority and being inspired directly by the Word of God to do so.

Of course, some deny that the Bible teaches healing, just as some deny that it says that Jesus is the Son of God. There is no Christian doctrine taught in the Scriptures which is not denied by some group. I find, however, that a good deal of sophisticated and complicated exposition of the Word is needed *not* to preach divine healing. It is such a straightforward truth. The golden rule of Bible interpretation is that usually the simple explanation is the most likely one, even in difficult passages. On the very surface, healing is a Bible truth. Healing passages are not even difficult, except when turned into controversy — the common strategy of those who don't believe what the Bible really says.

All this is exemplified in the healing of Jean Neil of Rugby, England. It stirred up an angry reaction from one or two whose pet theories were challenged. Mrs. Neil had suffered twenty-five years of physical trouble, sometimes getting better, but then being thrown back again, as when she was in a car crash and her spine was damaged. One day she had a dream so vivid she could remember every detail. She saw herself in a very large building, and a man was coming first to another woman in a wheelchair and then over to her.

For nearly two years she had more or less lived in a wheelchair. She might hobble a few steps by twisting from side to side; one limb was dislocated at the hip. She had worn a special medical corset to accommodate the distortion. Drugs had affected color-coordination in her eyes; she had heart attacks which left her with angina. Her spine had already been surgically fused and the coccyx removed. She suffered excruciating pain, sometimes screaming as she moved. Various specialists had treated her in hospitals. At that time she was deciding whether to undergo another critical and expensive operation on her spine. The surgeon said it could leave her worse or bring her no more than a degree of relief. Jean also had bronchitis, asthma and a hiatal hernia.

One day, a short time after her dream, she was taken with her husband to a rally in the Birmingham (England) National Exhibition Center. She looked around and recognized the place as the one in her dream. Some eleven thousand people were present and heard my salvation message. Afterward I went to minister to the sick and laid my hands first upon a wheelchair patient. Then God spoke to me and directed me right across this vast hall to minister to a woman at the side aisle — Mrs. Neil. I prayed and told her to stand, which she did uncertainly. Then suddenly, as she described it later, a great force went through her system. Within two minutes she had abandoned the confinement of her chair forever and was literally running around the place, jumping as if she had never had anything wrong with her. Every ailment in her body had instantly vanished.

Mrs. Neil has since traveled thousands of miles testifying to God's goodness. She took up jogging and swimming, and today, some six years later, she is a fit woman who never feels a single spasm of pain. The greatness of this miracle is seen in that although part of the spine had been surgically fused — and the work still shows on X ray — the specialist in charge of her care could find no impairment whatsoever of her movements. Total function has been restored.

One of the objections that arose from this cure was that we had published her story. It was asserted that if God works a miracle we must not testify about it in case it gives false hope to sufferers from similar afflictions. Well, the Bible itself strongly encourages testimony. "Let the redeemed of the Lord say so," Psalm 107:2 says. Scripture largely consists of testimony to the greatness of the works of God, and the intention is also clear — to encourage us to believe that the God of yesterday will do the same things today. The most positive grounds are laid down in countless passages that "the truth of the Lord endures to a thousand generations."

Criticism of Christ

It is disobedience to Christ not to minister healing. To raise the objection that not all are healed is a criticism of Jesus who commanded us to heal. He Himself delivered some, but passed by others, and He does the same now through His church.

Critics overlook something else, too. Healing is only a part or aspect of the responsibility to bring our petitions to God. Not all prayer is answered. There is no difference between asking for one thing and asking for another. If people don't pray for the sick because they may not be healed, are they going to be consistent and not pray for anyone in any kind of trouble in case nothing happens? Should we never ask God for anything so nobody's hopes will be dashed? After all, if we believe nothing, then we will not be disappointed, right?

In Western conditions, it is a miracle when miracles actually occur because of the prevailing winds of withering unbelief. Some whole nations are like Nazareth, where Jesus could do no mighty work.

When the sick are healed in my meetings, I hear people say, "Jesus is wonderful." When the sick are not healed in my meetings, I hear some say, "Bonnke is no good." I agree with them. If there is a fault it may be either mine or theirs, but Jesus never fails.

The Gift and the Gifts

Now we must come back to the phrase *gifts of healings*. We will ask a question first and that will lead us to a full explanation of the gift. Does it mean there are just so many healings earmarked for patients? No. First, remember that God is no respecter of persons (see Acts 10:34). James, brought up with Jesus as part of the family, was particularly impressed by Christ's undiscriminating concern. He says, "If you show favoritism, you sin and are convicted by the law as lawbreakers" (James 2:9, NIV). This was part of the "royal law" of the kingdom (v. 8), that we love our neighbors as ourselves. It is called the royal law because the king Himself acts on that principle.

Who then will receive healing? James helps us. "Has not God chosen the poor of this world to be rich in faith and heirs of the kingdom?" (James 2:5). Christ stressed the fact to John the Baptist that "the poor have the gospel preached to them" (Matt. 11:5). In Acts 3:1-8, Peter gave a gift of healing, saying to a cripple, "Silver and gold I do not have, but what I do have I give you: In the name of Jesus Christ of Nazareth, rise up and walk" (v. 6).

The Disenfranchised

Jesus had a profound feeling for the poor, but they were not the only deprived ones. Certainly Zacchaeus and other tax gatherers were rich. When Jesus preached in the synagogue at Nazareth He built up a picture of physical deliverance for people deprived because they were foreigners. He referred to a non-Jewish widow outside Israel territory to whom God sent the prophet Elijah. Jesus then went to the same Gentile area, Sidon, to another non-Jewish woman and brought healing into her home. Sidon had its own patron god of healing, Eshmon, and his temple, but he could do nothing for this woman whose daughter had a devil (Mark 7:24-30). She heard Jesus was there, and she determined to see Him. The disciples tried to get rid of her and even Jesus tested her, but she persisted until He eventually responded.

Christ's remark is famous: "Let the children be filled first, for it is not good to take the children's bread and throw it to the little dogs" (Mark 7:27). He describes people with rights and those without. The children were Israel, who had rights. To them belonged the promises and the covenant of God. The "dogs" were those outside the commonwealth of Israel.

To the children of the household bread is a right, their birthright. To those outside the household it is a gift, "tossed" to them as a favor. Jesus said that healing was the bread of the children of Israel. The woman quickly realized that what was not hers by right she could have as a gift and wittily summed it up by saying, "Yes, Lord, yet even the little dogs under the table eat from the children's crumbs" (v. 28). For her background and semiheathenism she displayed a grasp of God's universal goodness which is comparatively rare even two thousand years later.

Early evangelists used to hammer at their hearers, saying that if they wished to be healed they must first be saved from sin. They were both right and wrong. If people wished to come under the promises of healing then they must be saved. But they could be healed through the gifts of healings if they were not born-again children of God — if God willed it and if they could take the healing by the hand of faith. It rested on the graciousness of God.

Sometimes it has seemed that the unsaved are healed when believers are not. This could be, and Jesus commented on this. He declared that people would come from the east and west and sit down with Father Abraham while the children of the kingdom would be cast out. Believers can be unbelieving. Pastors explain the lack of healings under their ministry in terms which don't build up expectation. A sermon on "Six Reasons Why the Sick Are Not Healed" will not bring a line of expectant sick folk to the front. Negative teaching, sin or rank disobedience to the will of God calls for repentance first. Meanwhile, non-Christians with a simple outlook benefit by the gifts of healings. One thing is possible, namely that God in His goodness initiates miracles to encourage faith — that is, Bible teaching. So He may use the gifts of healings to help believers who may somehow have become bogged down in a non-faith situation.

The Word and Healing

Now look at the relation of the Word to healing. While Jesus did speak of healing as bread, He also spoke of the Word of God as bread. Healing is the Word of God in action! He taught us to pray, "Give us this day our daily bread" (Matt. 6:11). He also said, "Do not labor for the food which perishes, but for the food which endures to everlasting life" (John 6:27) — that is, the Word of God. We need that bread daily. It is the life-giving, healthful and healing Word of life. "Your word has given me life" (Ps. 119:50). "He sent His word and healed them" (Ps. 107:20). To those living daily by the bread of life, the bread of healing is no gift but is health imparted daily through their spiritual nutriment.

In my campaigns I do not preach healing, but I preach the Word of God, and it releases living faith. It is easy then for the Holy Spirit to move through a crowd and touch people with open hearts. "Seek first the kingdom, and these things will be added" (Matt. 6:33, paraphrase).

If we live by the Word, we shall find life in it. God said, "Man shall...live...by every word that proceeds from the mouth of God" (Matt. 4:4). Withdrawal of life (death because of sin) is reversed by the Word of life. "Every word" is not just a mouthful daily, but a good meal. The multitudes Christ fed with common bread didn't pay a penny — no offering baskets went around. Jesus said, "You give them something to eat," and that is exactly what they did. The bread multiplied miraculously in their hands as they moved around supplying the people. The church is commanded, "You give them something to eat." That something is the Word of God, for in that Word is health and life.

A believer may be sick through sin, as we read in 1 Corinthians 11. Sin blocks the healthy flow of life, appetite for the Bread of Life declines, and some suffer from spiritual anorexia — "[He] sent leanness into their soul" (Ps. 106:15). If the elders of the church attend upon such a person, their prayer of faith saves the sick (James 5:14-16). Those who have sinned and are languishing as if cut off from the rights of the kingdom of God can be healed and forgiven. That healing is a gift to them, to restore them to full kingdom privileges.

The Attack on Healing

All those who pray for the sick either privately or publicly will be offered as much discouragement as help. Unbelievers try to explain away healings. They have a few glib ways around them, and the same arguments pop up time and time again; patients were not sick were wrongly diagnosed or they suffered only from a psychosomatic ailment.

Let us face the fact that in a universe like ours it is ridiculous to say God can't heal the sick. How does anybody know He can't? Our knowledge is so limited. "My own suspicion," says atheist-scientist J.B.S. Haldane, "is that the universe is not only queerer than we suppose, but queerer than we can suppose."[1] We would have to know everything about it to know what cannot happen. We cannot adopt an attitude of personal infallibility, but there are individuals who make it their duty to inform mankind of their dogmas. But God does know everything, and He finds miracles quite possible.

There is a curious state of mind among unbelievers. When a miracle healing takes place, they say God could not have done it because it breaks the scientific laws. They believe in "mind over matter" and psychological processes. Can mind over matter break scientific laws while God can't? Can we believe in psychological omnipotence, but not in divine omnipotence? I believe God can do anything except fail.

Some of the healings commonly being seen as a result of prayer are very hard to duplicate by other means, including psychiatric and hypnotic cures which are notoriously unstable anyway. Nothing known in medical history equals some of the amazing happenings in our crusades and in churches worldwide, including the healing of those with congenital disorders, the blind, the crippled, the deaf, the diseased and those cruelly affected by accidents.

One thing I know: Nobody has found one positive statement in Scripture against divine healing. Instead, critics have had to turn to church history to claim that miracles ceased with the apostles. There are Christians who claim the Bible as their sole authority, yet to prove their doctrine that Jesus no longer heals they refer to church history.

The universal problem of suffering will eventually completely be solved according to Revelation 21:4: "And God will wipe away every tear from their eyes; there shall be no more death, nor sorrow, nor crying; and there shall be no more pain, for the former things have passed away."

We are not living in the millennium yet, nor an ideal world, for that is the great end toward which God is working out His purposes. Meanwhile, the whole creation groans together waiting for that age to come, as we read in Romans 8.

Bursts of glory from that coming day light up the sky like lightning. The Holy Spirit is working with the church as He once worked with Jesus. Each healing is like a laser beam cutting through the darkness of this world until the day dawns and Christ reigns. Until then — what? We fight the good fight of faith, aided by the mercy of God and the gift of the gifts of healings.

12

MIRACLES

We must not assume that the "working of miracles" is more miraculous than the other eight gifts in 1 Corinthians 12. They are all the manifestation of the Spirit. Of course, the rationalizing critics dismiss the idea that any of them are supernatural; they regard them as natural talents. What talent the working of miracles represents calls for an awful lot of juggling. If the miraculous is rejected, this chapter becomes an impenetrable mystery. The efforts of rationalistic scholars to produce a nonsupernatural Christianity have produced something that bears no resemblance to the palpitating energy and life of the gospel that carried the apostles into the pagan world two thousand years ago.

To get into this subject, I believe it would help greatly to think first about the challenging and thrilling references to the miracle power of God at work everywhere the gospel went. The New Testament is a miracle book and Christianity is a miracle faith. The working of miracles is mentioned three times in 1 Corinthians 12, in verses 10, 28 and 29.

Jesus is the captain of our faith. He lamented over Capernaum which had not repented despite His "mighty works," using the term three times (Matt. 11:20-23). The King James Version refers to "wonderful works" in Matthew 7:22 and reports of His "mighty works" astonishing the people of Nazareth (Matt. 13:54). Peter could remind the Jews that Christ had been "attested by God to you by miracles, wonders, and signs" (Acts 2:22). The "miraculous signs" by the hand of Philip amazed Simon the sorcerer in Samaria (Acts 8:6, NIV). It happened everywhere, such as in Galatia where there was the working of miracles (see Gal. 3:5). The scattered Hebrew Christians had "tasted...the powers [miracles] of the age to come" (Heb. 6:5): "God also bearing witness both with signs and wonders, with various miracles, and gifts of the Holy Spirit" (Heb. 2:4).

The Old Testament congregation of Israel, essentially a church in the wilderness, came into existence by prophetic miracle and was maintained supernaturally. Even then, with all the wonders of Exodus, it was only a shadow of the church of Christ Jesus, created as it was from the wounded side of the Redeemer and born of God, to be endowed with the Spirit of the ancient prophets. As Israel was led by the pillar of fire and cloud, the church moves in the Spirit.

What Are Miracles?

Whatever miracles may be, we must first understand the word *miracle* itself. The Bible word is more correctly referred to as powerful deeds. It is a key word, occurring some 120 times or so in the New Testament.[1] The Christian faith is all miracle, and any representation of it without the power of the Holy Spirit is dead.

In many cases we read of mighty deeds without any more details. The disciples were never sent out without adequate divine power, not even when Jesus was on earth (Matt. 10:1-3.) Before He left them to ascend to glory, He told them not to leave Jerusalem until they were endued with power *(dunamis)* from on high (Acts 1:4). This did occur (2:4). From that time on they always went with perfect assurance that they moved in the might of God. Paul said, "I know that when I come to you, I shall come in the fullness of the blessing of the gospel of Christ" (Rom. 15:29).

Generally, mighty deeds were healings and deliverance from demons. We see that from Acts 8:6 and 13 which says, "The multitudes...heeded the things spoken by Philip, hearing and seeing the miracles which he did. For unclean spirits, crying with a loud voice, came out of many who were possessed; and many who were paralyzed and lame were healed...Simon was amazed, seeing the miracles and signs which were done."

Two other Bible words to consider are authority *(exousia)* and power *(dunamis)*. Christian authority rests on power. The authority of the police, for example, would mean nothing unless backed by all the power of the state. Christ showed that He had the authority *(exousia)* on earth to forgive sins, but behind it was the power of redemption and His work on the cross. We gladly sing, "There is power, power, wonder-working power, in the blood of the Lamb."[2] This, we shall see, has a very important link with the gift of the working of miracles.

The phrase "the working of miracles" in 1 Corinthians 12:10 is literally the "operations of powers" *(energemata dunameon)*. It covers all varieties of signs and wonders, and is plural for multiple miracles. It does not specify one particular type of miracle.

In the Old Testament, miracles are mainly nature miracles, such as the plagues of Egypt and the crossing of the Red Sea, the miracles of Elijah and Elisha, and the moving of the sundial shadow in Isaiah. In the New Testament, Jesus alone did such things, turning water into wine, feeding thousands with a boy's luncheon, quelling the threat of the storm and so on. We are not told that the apostles themselves did any of these things. Healings of the sick and exorcisms were the main signs referred to as mighty wonders.

We will dig a bit deeper. The English word *miracle* seems to convey more to the average person than what the Bible says. Many take *miracle* to mean sheer fairy-tale magic, squaring the circle or making two plus two equal five — nonsense events. We get *miracle* from the Latin word *miraculum*, meaning "to wonder at." It relates more to the magic of mythology than Christianity. Too often English speaking people think of a miracle as that kind of thing, putting the Bible on the same level as mythology.

Whatever God has done in creation or may do in His sovereign omnipotence, we know that the promise of the baptism with the Spirit does not copy myths but what Scripture portrays. H.G. Wells's famous story "The Man Who Could Work Miracles" describes how he first made a candle float upside down with the flame burning downward and then went on to destroy the earth with his "faith." Christianity has nothing in common with fairy-tale fantasy. Everything Christ did and everything the gifts enable us to do are in line with divine and moral purpose, reflecting God's wisdom.

The King James Version often avoids the word *miracle* and prefers *mighty deeds*, or *mighty works*. There were signs and wonders produced by the working of powers, extraordinary happenings beyond human ability expressed in Romans 15:19 (KJV) as "mighty signs and wonders, by the power of the Spirit of God."

Greater Works

Now this gift of the workings of power has to be linked with Christ's promise in John 14:12, 16: "I tell you the truth, anyone who has faith in me will do what I have been doing. He will do even greater things than these, because I am going to the Father...I will ask the Father, and he will give you another Counselor" (NIV).

Jesus promised these greater works. Yet as far as we know, the disciples only performed normal healings, and not one of them exceeded Christ's healing ministry. None of them performed a stupendous wonder like the raising of Lazarus four days after his death. What were the "greater works"? To answer that we shall have to make a small detour.

Greater things and mighty deeds of power certainly included healings. The healings of Jesus were called works. But Paul classified gifts of healings separately. The list of gifts was not meant to be a strict separation of different operations, since they overlap, but he clearly had some difference in mind between miraculous healings and miracles.

Could it be raising the dead? Possibly, since that is not healing. However, it must be something else too, because the Corinthians are not said to have raised the dead, though they "[came] short in no gift" (1 Cor. 1:7), and many of them had died (11:30).

It would include creative wonders like making new eyes, ear drums or the repair of bones damaged by accident or osteoarthritis. The gifts overlap, and what we might call a healing on one occasion could be classified as a miracle on another. There are some curious occurrences, miraculous in the scientifically impossible sense. Cures take place where there seems to be no physical change, but function is inexplicably restored. An eye which still appears to be damaged suddenly has clear vision; hands that appear twisted with arthritis can be flexed and are free of pain; people walk who ought not to be able to walk.

For further help we turn to what Jesus promised about greater works. He Himself performed the greatest possible cures. Their magnitude was never exceeded by the apostles. Yet it was Christ Himself who spoke of His own disciples' exceeding the greatness of His works, doing greater works. It is quite obvious that it would have to be a different kind of divine wonder beyond what was ever seen in His ministry. Jesus' promise showed that these greater works would be accomplished by the power of the Holy Spirit (John 14:12-17).

Now notice that He repeated the same promise in Acts 1:4-5, 8. On that occasion He spoke of other works which were not healings. Jesus promised the disciples "power" (Acts 1:8), the same word *(dunamis)* that is in 1 Corinthians 12. But power for what? This power was for far more than healing. It was for one special duty: world evangelism. "You shall be witnesses to Me...to the end of the earth."

There was another display of divine power never really seen before Christ which was to be a prophetic sign of the end times — to "turn many to righteousness" (Dan. 12:3). There were no revivals in the Old Testament, as the Holy Spirit was not given. At best, only reformations took place by royal command.

That work of global evangelization called for the comprehensive working of God through His disciples which was sufficient to meet every demand and to battle the entire world in opposition. It was a work which Jesus did not carry out but left to those who followed Him. To bring deliverance to millions helpless in every bond of sin and to change the thinking of the entire world was something greater than was seen in the earthly ministry of Christ. Christian conversion is greater than any healing. Salvation is God's greatest work, the perfection of His power.

When Paul first came to Corinth, carrying out the witness task, he said he came "in weakness, in fear, and in much trembling" (1

Cor. 2:3). Some believe he was suffering from a recurrent infection such as malaria, a weakness picked up on his travels or from beatings and hardship. Yet he described his preaching as being a "demonstration of the Spirit and of power" (v. 4). The effect was that a Christian church of blood-washed believers existed amid the spiritual squalor of an idolatrous city.

God's power enabled Paul to carry on despite his bodily weakness. He admitted to a "thorn in the flesh" (2 Cor. 12:7) but triumphed over it by the mighty grace God gave him, "strengthened with all might, according to His glorious power, for all patience and longsuffering with joy" (Col. 1:11). He sees himself as an example of the power of God working in him "as dying, and behold we live" (2 Cor. 6:9), with the Lord saying, "My strength is made perfect in weakness" (12:9).

Here is that perfection of power indicated by Jesus as greater. Paul calls it "the all-surpassing power [which] is from God" (2 Cor. 4:7, NIV) — divine power manifested in the most perfect and superlative sense. He speaks of it as being in "earthen vessels," in fragile flesh, those men and women mocked and persecuted by a harsh and cruel age. The Corinthians obliged him to boast of the great things and "signs of an apostle," which Paul said was a foolish thing. He spoke of the power of God sustaining him under the most overwhelming pressures and enabling him to carry the gospel everywhere (2 Cor. 11). Paul says, "If I must boast, I will boast in things which concern my infirmity…for when I am weak, then am I strong" (11:30; 12:10, NIV).

The power so evident in one man, the apostle Paul, has since been seen on a world scale. The persistence of faith and the amazing endurance of Jesus' followers have come to be accepted as commonplace. Looking at Christian beginnings and at the subsequent opposition against the unarmed and defenseless followers of Jesus century after century and at this very hour (350,000 reported as martyrs in 1992) indicates that some extraordinary power has to be admitted. We have the miracle of the church — a compound of every kind of miracle. The "surpassing greatness" of divine power is seen more in the heroic endurance of believers and in the expansion of the church against all resistance than in any physical healing.

Jesus did speak of "he that believes" doing greater works. But there was a greater work done by the whole church. Most important, it carried the kingdom of God outside the borders of Israel and then to vastly more people worldwide than Christ in the flesh ever could address in the small land of Israel. Jesus spoke of His own anointing by the Spirit, which He constantly referred to as the Father's work, but He particularly related it to Isaiah 61:1, to "preach good tidings to the poor." That work is being done on a global scale which would have been physically impossible for Christ incarnate to accomplish.

Why did the Father send the Holy Spirit? Without question it was to make it possible to preach the gospel to every creature on earth. Paul describes it as "to bring the nations into the obedience of the gospel" (Rom. 16:26; compare 1:5). The consuming passion and work of Christ was "to seek and to save that which was lost" (Luke 19:10). Jesus was never just a wonder-worker. First and foremost, He was a Savior. It was that work which took Him to the cross. That was the ultimate and premier aim of His earthly life. It was not for some social good — just to feed multitudes — but for the redemption of mankind. That was uppermost in His mind. Any talk of greater works has to be in line with His own great work to save the lost. Salvation is the greatest labor and the greatest marvel God ever undertook.

Paul spoke far more of the saving power of God than of any physical miracle. He saw the cross producing the greatest wonders of all, men and women being made alive "who were dead in trespasses and sins" (Eph. 2:1). "My message and my preaching were not with wise and persuasive words, but with a demonstration of the Spirit's power" (1 Cor. 2:4, NIV). For what purpose? "So that your faith might not rest on men's wisdom, but on God's power" (1 Cor. 2:5, NIV). A miracle healing only confirmed the greater wonder, the gospel (1 Cor. 2:1-5). Writing to the Thessalonians he makes this comment, "Our gospel did not come to you in word only, but also in power, and in the Holy Spirit and in much assurance" (1 Thess. 1:5). He refers to this effect even before he again comments on the same power working "in spite of severe suffering" (1:6, NIV).

We have already remarked on the fact that the mightiest of the inspired prophets all failed to procure anything very much in the way of national repentance. The only success was perhaps that of Jonah in Nineveh, a non-Jewish city. His words frightened them into change, of course. But Isaiah was sent to "make the heart of this people dull, and their ears heavy, and shut their eyes" (Is. 6:10). All that the prophets spoke of was judgment with only the most distant rays of hope. They were sent to "overturn, overturn" (Ezek. 21:27, KJV). "I have sent to you all My servants the prophets, rising early and sending them...but they did not listen or...turn from their wickedness" (Jer. 44:4-5).

But as soon as Peter, the first preacher of the age of the long-promised outpouring of the Spirit, opened his lips, the impact was such that nobody had ever seen on earth before. Jesus' preaching had no such result. In fact, He spoke of Capernaum's unrepentance despite the miracles He had performed there. But to those who believed on Him He opened up a new prospect of greater things. He gave to Peter the keys of the kingdom. That is, Peter would be the first one to unlock the door of the kingdom by the keys. Those keys were the Word of the cross and the power of the Spirit. The glorious opening day of the age of the Spirit came on the day of

Pentecost. Immediately, three thousand came into the kingdom of God, pushing aside the old religious inhibitions.

There are several repetitions in some form or other of the Great Commission (see Matt. 28:16-20; Mark 16:15-20; Luke 24:46-49; Acts 1:8). In all of them, the idea of a supernatural power is spoken of primarily for the work of evangelism. There was never any thought in the New Testament but of a revival force attending the preaching of the gospel — if the unconverted were present to hear it, of course. The great work of God is salvatio. Nothing in all the Scriptures exceeds the value placed upon it, and they refer to it constantly. God is great because His salvation is great.

The words *workings of powers* are plural. This suggests a variety of operations. Evangelism included healings, as we read, "The Lord worked with them and confirmed his word by the signs that accompanied it" (Mark 16:20, NIV). The work of world redemption calls for many gifts, and the gift of miracles includes healings, endurance and the power of God to change the hearts of men and women. Every conversion is a work of power — a miracle of all miracles. The work of Jesus touched some lives, but those He sends reach multiplied masses; they see miracle after miracle among the most remote and depraved in the world. The lost are found and saved.

The Inexplicable Miracle

Some miracles seem to bring more than one gift into play. For example, let me tell you about Mrs. Heidi Tufte of Norway. I gave a banquet in Oslo, and Mrs. Tufte attended. While I was speaking, the Lord said to me, "Rebuke paralysis." I interrupted what I was saying and told the people that the Holy Spirit was telling me to rebuke paralysis. I did so in a few words and in the name of Jesus.

What I had not seen was that there was a woman at the back

of that big hall in a wheelchair — Mrs. Tufte. The moment I rebuked paralysis something shot through her system, and she later said she began "churning within" day and night. About a week later that she awoke one morning with strange sensations which frightened her; life was flowing through her previously lifeless limbs.

She jumped out of bed and began to cry. Her husband wanted to support her, knowing her paralyzed state, but it wasn't necessary. "I am healed!" she exclaimed. Overcome with joy, they embraced and dropped down on their knees to give thanks and glory to God.

The news spread across Norway like wildfire, and Mrs. Tufte received flower bouquets from people rejoicing with her from across the land. To this day she leads a normal life, perfectly healed.

Unbelief can be ingenious in its arguments, but this type of miracle disposes of some of the so-called explanations invented to avoid giving glory to God. This healing was not by suggestion from me, since I was not present and had never spoken to her. Nor was it self-suggestion, for she was asleep when the healing life began to course through her body; it woke her up. It disposes of the idea that it was merely a natural recession; in fact, her paralysis was a genetic fault. It was not coincidence. For it to occur within a week of my prayer after a lifetime of paralysis is beyond the realms of the wildest coincidence. This was no case of wrong diagnosis or mind over matter.

The gifts operating in such a remarkable cure would be discernment, faith and miracles, as well as authority, which is another gift not listed by Paul.

There is one other issue relating to the "working of mighty deeds." Every now and then the suggestion is made that the Spirit of God is a vast complex of power. Isaiah 11:2 says, "The Spirit of the Lord shall rest upon him, the Spirit of wisdom and understanding, the Spirit of counsel and might, the Spirit of knowledge and of the fear of the Lord." The Holy Spirit is all those Spirits in one Spirit.

Paul uses similar language in 1 Corinthians 12: many operations, one Spirit. Revelation 5:6 speaks of "the seven Spirits of God sent out into all the earth" — seven being the number of divine perfection.

We must always keep in mind that the Holy Spirit is God working on earth in human lives. His manifestations are diverse because, in the work of salvation, all manner of wonders are needed. Jesus spoke of the Spirit's anointing Him with a five-fold task of deliverance (Luke 4:18). In short, there is not a single situation among sinners in which the Spirit of God cannot manifest Himself in some appropriate form. His sufficiency meets His servants at the frontier of every new situation and task.

In Africa, we in the Christ for All Nations team have seen sights which only the greatest power in heaven or earth could produce, perhaps greater than any ever seen before, but not so great as will be seen in the future. Acres upon acres of people massed together: Muslims, animists and nominal Christians, all being touched by the Lord, surrendering to Him by thousands upon thousands, being healed and being baptized in the Spirit. They give up their fetishes, idols, stolen goods and witchcraft emblems, and become vigorous witnesses to Christ. State presidents are converted, and Parliaments echo the cry, "Jesus saves!" The whole thing is a miracle — "the working of miracles," not of one kind but whatever miracle is needed to meet the crisis of man without God. The miracle of souls redeemed by the preaching of the Word.

Compared to such tremendous scenes, what are such wonders as an axe head floating in water, fire from heaven or walking on the water? God is not a sensationalist. He has one primary concern: people — their welfare and destiny. That interest has to be the measure of all greatness and power.

13

PROPHECY

Today, prophecy is taking a premiere place in the charismatic scene far beyond any other endowment of the Spirit. Therefore, we need to hold it up to the mirror of the Word. We are in good company. Prophecy was the gift that Paul wanted them all to enjoy in Corinth. "Follow the way of love and eagerly desire spiritual gifts, especially the gift of prophecy" (1 Cor. 14:1, NIV).

In this wish he was especially thinking of gifts operating in services of worship. Obviously, prophecy and tongues and interpretation will be "for the common good" (1 Cor. 12:7, NIV) mainly when a congregation is in session.

The whole of 1 Corinthians 14 assumes that Paul is thinking

of gifts when the people congregate. Some verses state it. For example, "If...an unbeliever or uninformed person in" (v. 24); "Whenever you come together...for edification" (v. 26); "in the church" (v. 28); "another who sits by" (v. 30); "in all the churches of the saints" (v. 33). His great thought is the edifying of the church, especially by speech gifts. He throws gifts together in several lists, in no special order, but he always includes the gift of tongues which together with interpretation takes on the character of prophecy.

Again we should note exactly what Paul says: "The manifestation of the Spirit is given to each one for the profit of all: for to one is given the word of wisdom through the Spirit...to another prophecy" (1 Cor. 12:7-8,10). We would not distort what Paul meant if we called it a word of prophecy.

A prophecy is a manifestation, but again we have to be careful to distinguish between prophecy in its varied forms. If we refer to the gift of prophecy we ought to know precisely what it means. 1 Corinthians 12:10 simply says, "To another [is given] prophecy." The noun is singular. It is a manifestation of the Spirit of prophecy. Now that does not constitute a gift in the outright sense, the ability to prophesy anytime a subject wants — to make prophecies at will. No such power is handed over. It is not a personal presentation to anybody. All the *charismata* are still in the Spirit's control. But we shall see in what sense there is a gift of prophecy.

We are given this useful information that "the spirits of the prophets are subject to the prophets" (1 Cor. 14:32), but, of course, we can only prophesy by and in subjection to the Holy Spirit. Nevertheless, something is given, and the Greek word *didotai* is used here to show that, in a real sense, it is something given — that is, each utterance. That giving, however, must be understood in the sense of the whole context of 1 Corinthians and not as a complete gift in our common modern sense.

We can put it this way: with all vocal gifts, the will of God and the will of man come together in harmony. While prophecy is not uttering glibly whatever enters our heads anytime we want and prefacing it with "I, the Lord, do say unto thee," it is also true that the Lord encourages the bold prophet who steps out in faith and initiative. The principle here is that the prophet is the servant of the Holy Spirit; the Spirit is not the servant of a prophet, but the Spirit works with the prophet. The Spirit does so because people are tied by time and circumstance.

Paul in these scriptures makes much of prophecy. He says we should all pray that we may prophesy and adds, "I wish you all spoke with tongues, but even more that you prophesied" (1 Cor. 14:5). The churches of Jesus are prophetic institutions. They exist because of the work of the Holy Spirit, who is "the spirit of the prophets." All church activity should be by the Spirit and in the Spirit. The Spirit of prophecy should characterize every church and its gatherings. That does not mean there must be constant spectacular display, but the prophetic Spirit should charge the hearts of all concerned. The scholar James Dunn puts it starkly, "Without prophecy the community cannot exist as the body of Christ; it has been abandoned by the Lord."[1]

The False

The subject of prophecy is ancient and vast. It calls for discrimination and judgment. The true and the false are not always easy to discern. That was so even long before the Christian age. It was certainly so in apostolic times, and it has been ever since. A great deal of prophesying has always tended to make prophecy commonplace, and some have always despised it. The people listened to Ezekiel as if they were listening to a pleasant song, he complained. Even the apostles showed some hesitation, insisting on proof that they were genuine. "Don't quench the Spirit, don't despise prophecies, but prove all things, hold fast the good, from every form of evil abstain" (1 Thess. 5:19-21, literal translation).

It is a tremendous claim to say that one speaks in the name of the Lord. We should not believe it just because somebody claims to do so. We should check the credentials of all who profess to be prophets and even then check their prophecies. Uncritical hearing is disapproved of in Scripture. Jesus said, "Consider carefully how you listen" (Luke 8:18, NIV).

Human nature approves what it likes to hear — "smooth sayings" (Is. 30:10, KJV), as in the last days of the Judean kings whose household prophets always gave optimistic (but wrong) predictions. Occasionally, Christian bodies have accepted prophecies simply because they confirmed their theological or organizational dogmas; thus, prophecies are prejudged, rather than judged. An honest search of Scripture is the only way. We must not ignore the simple rule: "By the mouth of two or three witnesses the matter shall be established" (Deut. 19:15). Prophecy has been misused to stifle dissident opinion, as when Jeremiah was put in a pit for disagreeing with the rest of the so-called prophets. We cannot test prophecy by ballot or majority opinion. *Vox populi* is rarely *vox Dei*. (The voice of the people is rarely the voice of God.)

The long history of disaster serves as an example and confirms warnings by Christ and the apostles to treat prophetic utterances with caution. We must always check them against the Word of God. We are always responsible for what we do, even if we are obeying somebody else's prophecy. Eve found that being deceived did not make wrong right. The results of false prophesying boomerangs on the deceiver.

Prophesiers moved around the early churches. Many believers were illiterate, the churches were young, and there was little Christian writing or experience to guide them. Teaching was needed, and prophets were welcomed. They arrived announcing their own inspiration, and it is not surprising that they were given great credence. For those scattered groups of early believers needing teaching, beggars could not be choosers.

All the apostolic leaders faced this problem, including John. He laid down one test — unless prophets taught that Christ had come in the flesh, they were not to be entertained or given hospitality (see 1 John 4:1-3). This particular rule was needed locally because the idea was becoming prevalent that God could never submit to crucifixion; only a phantom Christ could be crucified, never God. He only seemed to be real. This teaching was called docetism.

That was one error drifting in on the prevailing religious winds. There are signs that this teaching affected the Corinthians, whose claims to be "spiritual" meant they were familiar with deeper levels of life, believing even their flesh was now different and that they had already passed through resurrection. Paul met this dangerous nonsense in chapter 15 by speaking of the resurrection of the body. Teachings like this spread by prophetic claims gave apostolic leaders much anxiety.

Even in Moses' time tests had to be laid down (Deut. 13). Jeremiah also particularly challenged false prophets. While it is true that Israel's prophets were unique, all the nations had prophets or those considered inspired, such as the oracles at Delphos, Dodona and Delosi, and the guardians of the Sibylline Books. In the temples of this or that god there were women sitting on tripods who were reputed to be in communication with deities. They often jabbered in an occult trance or ecstasy. Priests claimed to be able to interpret the usually ambiguous prophecies.[2]

There is an instance of this in 1 Kings 22:15. Micaiah was asked by the king to prophesy about the proposal to attack Syria. At first he responded to the king with what the king wanted to hear, but it was ambiguous. "Go and prosper, for the Lord will deliver it into the hands of the king." King Ahab thought it would fall into his hands, but in fact it fell into the hands of the king of Syria.

Prophets were common enough. The schools of the prophets were a vital element in Israel; no doubt we owe to them much that was preserved and written down as Scripture. But after the Babylonian exile (590 B.C.), the role of prophet became less evident and even suspect. Prophets "speaking comfortable things" had let Israel down, and absolute national catastrophe was the result (Zech. 1:13ff). Nobody was anxious "to put on a [prophet's] robe of coarse hair to deceive," as Zechariah said after the Jewish exile (13:4-5). They were "ashamed" to assume the prophetic mantle. John the Baptist's call was so real that he did wear typical prophetic garb.

Abuse of spiritual gifts has been a major calamity in the church. If what we read about the Montanists of the second century is true (although we only have writings from their enemies), they made irresponsible claims of the Holy Spirit's speaking and proclaimed false predictions of the kingdom of God being set up in Phrygia. This led to a tradition in the church that frowned on spiritual manifestations and excitement. It was considered fanatical "enthusiasm." This was perhaps one of the saddest and most damaging church decisions of all time. The bishops, of course, feared that if the Spirit spoke through laypeople, their authority could be undermined. The possible excesses of the Montanists gave them the excuse they needed to suppress what was going on.

History confronts us with a heartbreaking series of pseudo-prophets and demon-inspired teachings which has damaged the church beyond all telling. It would be impossible to think of anything that needs to be treated with greater caution. False prophecy has filled the world with error, unorthodox sects and false world religions. The prophetic trend in the church is strong at present, but to build on it as a foundation for the church without constantly checking it by the plumbline of the Word of God would leave an unstable structure at best. Only the Word of God provides a sound foundation for the "church of the living God, the pillar and ground of the truth" (1 Tim. 3:15). A church led by prophets will be misled sooner or later. The maxim is "Should not a people inquire of their God?" (Is. 8:19, NIV). The answer is yes, but "to the law and to the testimony! If they do not speak according to this word, they have no light in them" (v. 20, NIV).

"When men tell you to consult mediums and spiritists, who whisper and mutter, should not a people inquire of their God?" (Is. 8:19, NIV). People "consult the dead on behalf of the living"; why should they not consult God? The long history of imposters, charlatans, occultists, cult leaders and false and self-deceived ecstatics does not mean there is no true divine inspiration. On the contrary, it proves there must be the real; counterfeit coins can only copy the genuine. The devil would not neglect such a strategy. He made it his work even from the beginning in Eden to offer a counterfeit prophecy, leaving the pair uncertain of the voice of God. He will deploy his own inspired agents to unsettle those who hear the Word of God. These are the birds that devour the seed of the sower (see Matt. 13:4).

The Real

The Bible cuts a path through the tangle of prophetic claims and shows us the real. The whole Bible is a prophecy. It moves onward to a climax.

The Old Testament consists of three sections called the Law, the Prophets and the Writings. The Prophets includes historical books. They are part of the unfolding revelation of the ultimate aims of God. God's intentions began to be indicated way back in Genesis 1:27-28: "God created man in his own image, in the image of God he created him; male and female he created them. God blessed them" (NIV). In Genesis 3:15 God said to the serpent who deceived Eve, "I will put enmity between you and the woman, and between your offspring and hers; he will crush your head, and you will strike his heel" (NIV). This looked far ahead to Christ and His final triumph.

The call of Abraham pointed to far-off divine plans to bless all the families of the earth. Abraham "saw" Christ's day and looked beyond to the eternal city of God (Gen. 12:1-3; John 8:56; Heb. 11:10). All prophecy, including the gift, should move in that same all-important direction, to focus the hopes, faith and conduct of us all toward the realization of eternal redemption and the kingdom.

We need to be aware that prophecies may be trivial even when they are delivered in resounding and dramatic tones. They can be side issues, unrelated to the wider interests of the kingdom and what God is contemplating. Prophecy not born from the womb of God's plan of redemption is worthless. It is in the value category of palmistry and the horoscope. Somebody has said, "If a prophecy is not of God, it is too slight to be proved, and if it is of God it ought not to be proved." That is flawed logic. We need to know whether it *is* of God; that is what testing is all about.

Prophecy is a manifestation of the presence of God and therefore places hearers before God. It challenges our direction and brings pressures upon us to move only in accordance with His actions.

One of the finest descriptions of the true prophet actually comes from that alien and strange character, Balaam, in Numbers 24:4. He says he is one who "hears the words of God, who sees the vision of the Almighty, who falls down, with eyes opened wide." (The KJV says "into a trance," but the words are not in the original manuscripts.) "The vision of the Almighty" refers to God's vision for mankind, and Balaam found he could say nothing except in line with God's future for Israel.

The great prophetic book of the New Testament is Revelation. It gives a unique panorama of the grand divine scheme, drawing together elements from all the previous prophecies. It begins, "The Revelation of Jesus Christ, which God gave Him to show His servants — things which must shortly take place" (1:1). If the spirit of any prophecy cuts across the general scheme of biblical revelation and the purposes of God in the gospel, but does not relate to these in any sense, then little weight should be attached to it. Either it is devilish or, more likely, of human imagination.

Prove All Things

A prophet whose words come to pass might be more dangerous than one whose word does not come to pass. The test of a true prophet is not that his words come to pass. Satanic forces can organize that also. Deuteronomy 13:1-5 warns us, "If a prophet...announces to you a miraculous sign or wonder, and if [it]...takes place, and he says, 'Let us follow other gods...you must not listen...That prophet or dreamer must be put to death" (NIV). The evidence that a prophecy is not true becomes apparent, of course, when it fails to come to pass. "How can we know when a message has not been spoken by the Lord? If what a prophet proclaims in the name of the Lord does not take place or come true, that is a message the Lord has not spoken. That prophet has spoken presumptuously. Do not be afraid of him" (Deut. 18:21-22, NIV).

Even a true man of God can speak from his own mind and be mistaken. There is a difference between a false prophet and one who speaks presumptuously. A false prophet brings false teaching.

A failed prophecy merely shows a man is speaking out of himself. Nathan spoke out of his own mind when he told David that he should go ahead and build the temple. Later he had to correct this mistake and brought God's own mind to David (not to build). Isaiah told Hezekiah he would die, but he had to return almost at once with a different message that he would live. In several places Paul heard prophecies which he did not accept; those prophecies were not infallible.

There is such a thing as prophesying according to the proportion of our faith. When God spoke to me to build the world's largest gospel tent to seat thirty-four thousand people, I met with the brethren of my board to discuss it. After we had discussed the matter we prayed together; one of the men present began to prophesy. He began, "Thus saith the Lord, 'Thousands shall be saved under this roof.'" Then he stopped and said to us, "Excuse me. This is not what the Holy Spirit said; I didn't have the faith to utter it. Let me start again. Thus says the Lord, 'Millions will be saved under this roof.'"

How right he was, but it was not just under the canvas roof. The tent would have to be filled for many years to house enough unconverted people to amount to millions of conversions. But a work was beginning under that roof which would continue under the canopy of the glory of God as we moved across the African continent where we actually witnessed those millions of precious people being saved.

There are prophets who credit to themselves special authority to impose their ideas upon others. They even believe that their own interpretation of Scripture is given by revelation and is not to be challenged. One teacher asserted, "God has told me what such-and-such a scripture means," even though it was a distorted interpretation. If we are to prove all things, we cannot let such claims to authority go unchallenged. Of all people, the prophet

181

must submit to the judgment of others. A prophet's own claim that he speaks by the word of the Lord is not enough. God has left authority with the churches. Jesus told us to beware of such dogmatists.

Anyone bringing "a word from the Lord" should realize what that means — that it is an implicit claim to be a prophet according to Scripture. They ought to be really sure that God has spoken before they speak. A person claiming to be a prophet who is nothing of the kind is an abomination in the sight of God.

Mechanics of Prophecy

Some prophecy is in the first person — "I, the Lord, do say unto thee...." This is an awesome claim. Sometimes it is proved not to be the Lord God speaking, but only Jack or Mary. A man may claim he is "standing in the counsel of the Lord." Let it be recognized that this claims an exclusive distinction above other believers. We all have the Word of God which is the counsel of the Lord in which we stand. Even considering the gifts of wisdom, knowledge and prophecy, Paul could say to the Corinthians, "The spiritual man makes judgments about all things, but he himself is not subject to any man's judgment: 'For who has known the mind of the Lord that he may instruct him?' But we have the mind of Christ" (1 Cor. 2:15-16, NIV). It is therefore hardly legitimate for one man to place himself on a higher level than all believers who "have the mind of Christ."

There is the question of language in prophecy. Often the English lapse into the three hundred-year-old form of their tongue found in the King James Version of the Bible. Actually, it was becoming dated even when that Bible first appeared. It is a tradition copied from one to another through the decades, especially by people who were deeply versed in the King James Version. But it should not detract from the value of what is said. The reason prophecy is often couched in this style is because it is filtered through our minds — which as far as religion is concerned has come to us from the Word of God in Elizabethan form. It is a religious habit of speech often heard in prayer, as in the *Anglican Book of Common Prayer*. But it is the picture, not the frame, that matters.

We can use everyday speech, which certainly was always the case in Bible days. What is not good is to dress up uninspired spiritual cliches in a majestic literary style hoping to sound like Isaiah in full flight, prefaced by "I, the Lord, do say unto thee." If our word is from the Holy Spirit we need not try to make it appear so.

The Old Testament Prophet and the New Testament Prophet

The designation "prophet" covers all manner of inspired speakers, even the false. The Old Testament prophet is not the same as the New Testament prophet. In fact, Christ said that the prophets prophesied until John the Baptist, indicating that was the end of an era (Matt. 11:11-13). Some differences can be mentioned.

The pre-Christian prophet was God's mouthpiece to those who had no direct contact with the Lord. What the Lord had to say was revealed to the prophets, and through them to Israel, and to some outside Israel. Individuals as well as the nation had access to the will of God through the prophet or through the high priest if he had the Urim and Thummim. Even the Edomites could have had that access (Is. 21:12).

The Hebrew prophets were lone figures. The Pentecostal or charismatic who prophesies is not — but is — part of the prophetic group, the church. They all know the Lord, and they do not need anybody to stand between them and God. They are God's new covenant people in a new relationship, and they "know the Lord" (Heb. 8). No one needs to enquire of the Lord on another's behalf.

We have said elsewhere that there is no conception of higher or lower but of one body with many parts. Some may be leaders, which gives them prominence but not superiority. Those they lead are playing their own roles and are therefore not inferiors but equals in God's sight. *Office* is read into passages in the New Testament relating to elders and deacons, but no such word or intent is there. The thought is always function, not position. "Clothe yourselves with humility toward one another" (1 Pet. 5:5, NIV). This applies to the prophet as well as anybody else. There is no office of prophet to which a believer can be officially appointed. Prophets are not judged on whether they are commissioned by men or not.

There is no place for an intermediary between men and the Holy Spirit when all are Spirit-energized and gifted as "a royal priesthood" (1 Pet. 2:9) "Call no man Master," Jesus said. "Be shepherds, not lording it over those entrusted to you" (1 Pet. 5:2-3, NIV). There is no hierarchy, for all are servants of all, and in Christ there is neither male nor female. The laity do not depend on an elite authority, for all have charismatic or apostolic powers. The pastor who does not delegate will see the limbs of the body deteriorate. A denominational leader once demanded that only evangelists with experience should evangelize. But how can a man get experience unless he evangelizes?

Believers under the new covenant are not to be directed in their lives through any third party. "Those who are led by the Spirit of God are the sons of God" (Rom. 8:14, NIV). That is our royal privilege and freedom. To assert the right of delegated authority and to delegate authority over to others is contrary to the kingdom principle and is precisely in step with the present secular world system. Jesus never directed people's decisions, not even His own disciples. He gives us freedom, and whatever advice we take or whomever we obey, we are responsible for what we do, prophecy or no prophecy.

The prophets of Israel often spoke to the whole nation. The New Testament prophet does not. Actually, the Hebrew prophets before Christ spoke to the nation as God's people, and the Christian prophet speaks to the church as God's people. No New Testament figure after John the Baptist went as Jeremiah or Amos did, with a commission to address national affairs. In the time of the kings of Israel some prophets, such as Nathan, were retained in some kind of official capacity for this purpose of national guidance. Samuel and the charismatic judges acted as national leaders, but there is nothing like this in the Christian dispensation.

The voice of God to the nations today comes through the whole body of the church. What Isaiah was to Israel, the whole church is to Germany, Britain or America. The church's existence, way of life and principles of service should be a constant challenge to the ways of nations. When the church ceases to bring God's vision to a nation, calamity is near. That is why the church must be charismatic. All who led early Israel were charismatic until Solomon. The weakness of Israel after this was that they had a Davidic dynasty but not a Davidic charismatic anointing.

The prophet in the apostolic church was not a fixed office, nor were apostles, teachers, evangelists or pastors. God gave people of that type to the church, whether they were given recognition or not. Men may appoint, but only God can endow, and God gives little heed to our arbitrary choices or elections. What any church should do is set out in Acts 13, namely to separate men to the work "to which God has called them" (v. 2). Unfortunately, jealousy that God has called or gifted an individual has often frustrated their call. Those in leadership have sometimes closed the doors of opportunity to God's own chosen, just as Saul opposed David. If a prophet may not be appointed, he should at least be recognized.

A prophet should also be known. That is implicit in 1 Corinthians. For a stranger to invade worship and address everybody uninvited is not merely discourteous, but out of order. There are those whose names are unfamiliar to us and who prophesy by mail, in printed circulars or magazines. Prophecies come from organizations (can an organization prophesy?), but unless readers of these emotional outbursts know who the prophets are and what their credentials are, they can be disregarded. Isaiah we know; Paul we know; but who are they?

How Does Prophetic Utterance Come?

The first essential is the sense of the Spirit's drawing or leading us in that direction. The sense of the prophetic spirit moving us may come even before we know what the "burden of the Lord" is. The prophets were called to speak and then given the message later (Is. 6; Jer. 1). One cannot speak from a cold heart. Someone speaking with tongues may bring to us an instant leading to interpret. Some prophesiers need that stimulus and never otherwise speak. In that case their gift is interpretation.

The word of God may come to us as a gradual growing of a burden from the Lord or as a flash of brilliant illumination. It can be in the mind as words, a thought, a significant picture, a vision, a dream, an inner conviction or an impulse, but it will be expressed in words. Sometimes it will seem that the process is instantaneous, the thought and the words flowing together extemporaneously, as if from outside oneself.

We cannot "work up" the voice of God within us, nor can we think it up. It comes from heaven. That is true, but how and when we give it is entirely our own responsibility. It can be written down and read to those whom God shows us. Isaiah and Jeremiah were writing prophets. It might be far better expressed with that kind of care. We even read of Elijah's sending a prophecy by letter.

The leader of a church or service is there to keep a decent orderliness and also to ensure that no wrong teaching is given. To throw open a meeting to virtually anyone is almost a tradition in many assemblies, and the risks it carries are only too wellknown. Some leaders fail to recognize their responsibility, and they let anything go. Certain situations call for rectification by the graciousness of the Lord. In the case of prophecies, at least, this is scriptural. In larger churches it becomes necessary to check prophecies which may be given beforehand, or at least evaluate the prophesiers. This avoids the possibility of the proceedings becoming a chaotic affair. It is a commended practice today that prophecies are submitted to the pastor to "test all things; hold fast what is good" (1 Thess. 5:21). Then they can be given at an appropriate time during worship and, if necessary, made audible by use of sound equipment. Otherwise, what is spontaneous can become disorderly.

Speaking with tongues is characteristically spontaneous, however. Paul realized this and offered guidelines for tongues as well as for prophecy. He put it that one speaker should speak at a time, only twice or three times at the most. He knew how some would dominate the worship. We are to excel in the manifestation of the Spirit and use wisdom in all things. Some pastors insist that permission to speak with tongues must be given. This avoids anything which is out of keeping with what is going on, but it does create a big risk that the spirit of the prophets is dampened down altogether. To "quench not the Spirit" (1 Thess. 5:19, KJV) often calls for a lot of wisdom and loving tact.

Prophets and Prophesiers

It will help students of the gifts if we say that we must differentiate between prophets and those who prophesy. Our lack of language in the realm of such things makes that easier said than done. There are no criteria in the New Testament to help us discriminate between prophets and those who prophesy. Presumably those who frequently prophesy may be called prophets, but we are short of words to make rigid distinctions. Paul calls all prophesiers "prophets" in 1 Corinthians 14:29,32, but even in his thinking a difference seems to exist. He seems to place those who prophesy often and those who have the normal signs following spoken of in Joel 2:28 ("your sons and daughters shall prophesy") in different categories. That's why he asks, "Are all prophets?" (1 Cor. 12:29). We read that Philip had four daughters who prophesied — it shuns calling them prophetesses, though this may reflect the age when women were not as free as today.

Not only prophesiers but also tongues-speakers, those healing and working miracles and others with gift ministries are not given a distinctive name. Prophecy by someone who is regularly heard or by someone only occasionally heard is the same and equally valuable. A healing by the laying on of hands of an elder does not mean he has the gift of the gifts of healings but is as much a sign of God's love as a healing by the mightiest healer in the world.

God does not distribute titles and medals. Nobody does anything except by the Holy Spirit. What glory can there be to a man? I have as much to do with healings taking place in my crusades as an electric teakettle has to do with a nuclear generator. The church has every characteristic since it has the Holy Spirit, but each member has his or her own gift. It is all an organic and charismatic work, but God "gives them to each one, just as he determines" (1 Cor. 12:11, NIV).

14

DISCERNMENT

The gift of discernment is not a natural knowledge of people's psychology, much less the power to "see through" everybody and to make the sensational discovery that all human beings are imperfect.

Again, let's note exactly what is said. The NIV speaks of "distinguishing between spirits" where the KJV has "discerning of spirits" (1 Cor. 12:10). The Greek word for discerning, *diakriseis*, comes from the Greek *krino*, which is a verb translated "to judge." It covers a wide field. It is not the gift to see what is invisible — a demon for example — but the power to judge what is seen, whether good or bad (see Heb. 5:14). The thought is that of separating one thing from another.

A form of the word *diakresis* is also used in the following examples:
- Judging between brothers (1 Cor. 6:5)
- Judging ourselves (11:31)
- Judging prophecies (14:29)

These have nothing to do with the gift of discernment.

We get our word critic from the same root, and it is found in Hebrews 4:12: The Word of God is a "discerner of the thoughts and intents of the heart" (KJV). The New International Version says, "It judges the thoughts," which is more correct. It means to discriminate or differentiate.

From this it is clear that the main meaning is not seeing demons, but judging what is visible and audible. The gift is not sight, but discrimination. It is true that the experience of "seeing" or sensing demons which may be concealing their presence (which they usually do) is not uncommon among Christian believers. In a general sense, this gift may include such discernment, but not necessarily. One can have experiences for which no gift is listed.

Next, we should note that the word is plural: discernments. That is, it is not a general gift of discrimination but comes as repeated manifestations as God grants them when needed, as with all gifts or revelations of the Holy Spirit. While the Spirit may use anybody anytime, these judgments are often specially given to one individual — we then say they have the gift.

In fact, we are told that others must exercise discrimination about prophecies (1 Cor. 14:29). This does not always need the gift of discernment, though without this gift we could make a mistake and condemn what should be welcomed. The gift is not merely to recognize what is spiritually evil, but also what is good. The Spirit of the Lord rested on David, but his brethren did not want to know. The blessed of the Lord are not always an immediate hit with their friends or colleagues!

There are rules by which everybody can judge prophecy and other matters. Usually, no supernatural help is needed to "discern" when a person has a demon — it is obvious. The Spirit of all gifts is in the church, and there His manifestations of one kind or another are part of the ongoing ministry of the church, such as healing, tongues and faith. Particular individuals have a marked ministry in some aspect of the Spirit and so are said to have a gift. Discernment, or, more correctly, the power to judge spirits, has to be very evident throughout the body of the church.

The word Paul uses in 1 Corinthians 12:10 means to differentiate between spirits. The same thing is in 1 John 4:1-3, though a different word is used *(dokimazete,* "to prove"). John writes, "Every spirit that confesses that Jesus Christ has come in the flesh is of God" (v. 2). That is his simple test for one form of false teaching. I know it sounds as if there may be many spirits which are of God, but John is not saying that. When spirits seem to be saying that Christ came in the flesh, it is the (one) Spirit of God speaking. "By this you know the Spirit of God" (v. 2). The word *spirit* is used in a broad sense of spiritual manifestations. Actually, in this case, John mainly had in mind an error that was creeping in — later known as gnosticism — which said the body of Christ on the cross was only a phantom. John does not mention any gift for discerning spirits but gives a simple test anybody can apply. He does, however, insist on the connection with this: "You have an anointing from the Holy One, and you know all things" (1 John 2:20), which does indicate a supernatural discernment.

The gift of discernment overlaps with a word of wisdom, but especially concerns spirits. We are told in many places to evaluate what is said or done. Believers are not to swallow everything they hear, especially things which purport to be from the Lord or are declared to be God speaking. Uncritical acceptance of so-called prophecies, claims to knowledge and revelation without proper evaluation, is regarded as foolish in Scripture. Unfortunately, it is common. It is astonishing how naive many are. We constantly see people being deceived, sometimes only in marginal matters, but often in real error with fearful results — countless new cults and fanaticism which can lead to tragedy and death.

In the field of the supernatural gifts, this one is vital. There are counterfeits being passed as genuine — hence the remark about "doctrines of demons" (1 Tim. 4:1) and human imitations that require the gifts to be subject to judgment. It is the burglar alarm for intruders in the realm of the supernatural gifts. Some have seen a certain logical sequence in the Corinthian list. Certainly putting discernment first seems wise.

The gift of discernment covers the widest field of spiritual interests, not just one small item of discernment of the devil. It is certainly needed in everything, especially prophecy and other teaching about which we are so often warned in Scripture. Demons do 99 percent of their work unseen without manifesting themselves. We have to be sensitive to the "doctrines of demons" (1 Tim. 4:1) which come as new revelation.

The voice of the Spirit is often very quiet. The agitation of our own passions and motives can drown it out. Jesus' temptations in the wilderness were remarkable because in each one He was tempted to do what seemed to be good for mankind; it was even backed up by Scripture! But He saw the subtlety of Satan each time. It is more important to judge new teachings than to look for demons in everybody.

Perceiving Demons

There are various ways this gift has been understood. Ralph Martin, noted author and professor of New Testament at Fuller Theological Institute, refers to it as the power to judge prophecies and demonic substitutes. D.G. Dunn is a scholar who thinks it is a form of prophecy used as a check against the abuses of other gifts, not merely to judge prophecies as commanded in 1 Thessalonians 5:20-21. It has been seen as "the Spirit-given ability to distinguish the Spirit of God from a demon spirit under whose direction the charismatic exercises a particular gift."[1]

Another writer regards it as a gift to free pastoral life from influences which do not come from God; to build up the church. It is doctrinal discernment — making correct, subjective value judgments — perhaps of a gift operating in the whole community. All of these suggestions may well be part of the answer, as Paul only names this gift and does not explain it. One thing is certain: It provides protection against what is spiritually false.

The gift of discernment has been related to the three tests of charismatic happenings in 1 Corinthians 12-14:

- That tongues and prophecies never say Jesus is accursed (1 Cor. 12:3).
- They are marked by love (1 Cor. 13:4-7).
- They build up the church (1 Cor. 14:12).

These Bible principles of judgment are not supernatural tests, obviously; but the gift of discernment is supernatural and needs to be. There are so many ideas, voices and teachings entering our minds or thrown up by our own thoughts that need the discerning eye of God Himself to distinguish good from bad. Our own hearts can mislead us, for it is "deceitful above all things" (Jer. 17:9). There are signs and wonders, prophecies and much more phenomena that could "deceive...even the elect," as Jesus warned us in Matthew 24:24.

The gift of discernment can save us from deception, though the Word of God also has that work to do as a "discerner of the thoughts and intents of the heart" (Heb. 4:12). Many deceptions are successful because believers understand so little of the Word of

God. Our own will, the deviousness of our hearts and the trickery of the enemy all need to be exposed. The Spirit of God can make us sensitive to the approach of what is or is not of God. "My sheep hear my voice" (see John 10:3,16). There is even such a thing as failing to discern what is holy, as some do not "discern the Lord's body" (see 1 Cor. 11:29).

Albert-Marie Besnard says that "members of the Renewal are more and more frequently tending to see demons at work in everything that is no more than human." It is a remarkable gift to discern demons where there are no demons. It is an attempt to imitate the gift of discernment, or at least to activate it by one's own thought and ordinary powers of critical judgment. That is not the gift of discernment.

We never read in the New Testament of anyone's discerning demons in people's lives. That does not invalidate such experiences, however. From the beginning, Peter perceived that Ananias and Sapphira were liars (Acts 5:1-11). Then Simon Magus, a sorcerer practicing magic and the black arts, wanted to buy the power of God. Peter said, "I see that you are poisoned by bitterness and bound by iniquity" (Acts 8:23). The apostle said nothing about demons. To put Simon right, Peter cast no demon out of him, but simply told him to repent of his wickedness and ask God to forgive him. Simon then asked Peter to pray for him (Acts 8:9-25). These instances may be classified as discernment, prophecy or a word of knowledge. Everything that the Holy Spirit does cannot possibly be categorized under nine gifts.

Because of the mention of this gift, some go looking for demons to cast them out. It has been argued that we must take the initiative in aggression, find the demons and attack them. Paul certainly did nothing like that. He cast out a demon of divination from a fortune-teller slave girl (Acts 16:18). It needed no discernment, as demon possession rarely does. Everybody in the city knew she had a spirit, and for days Paul refused to go on the attack against the power of darkness. But she pestered him so much that he felt people might associate her and her spirit of divination with the gospel and suppose that it was one of Paul's teachings. What he did discern was that she was doing his work no good.

The same thing happened with Jesus. Unclean spirits knew Him and said who He was, but Jesus commanded them to be silent (Mark 1:23-26, 34). He wanted no recommendation from them. He wanted nobody to be misled into thinking that demons were his friends or that they went along with Him. He cast them out. They were trying to "jump on the bandwagon" as if He had come from some general world of spirit.

The Lord Himself, the disciples and Philip all cast out demons. People came to them or were brought to them for that purpose, obviously because they knew that they were possessed. The presence of a demon is usually too appalling to miss, although the devil does not always make himself conspicuous. On the contrary, occult and physical activities advertise his presence too much and cause him trouble. He prefers to walk in the dark or to masquerade as an angel of light. In fact, those who have tried to be possessed or "have" a spirit or spirit guide don't always find it that easy.

Normally, the powers of darkness prefer to work undercover. For example, Jesus predicted "great signs and wonders, so as to deceive, if possible, the very elect" (Matt. 24:24). Even those with a familiar spirit or spirit guide don't rave like the Gadarene madman out of whom Jesus cast a legion of spirits which were tearing him in every direction (Luke 8:26-39). Nevertheless, unclean presences often cling to those who try to deal with these dark spirits and those who try to contact the dead.

The gift of discernment is given for other deceptions as well.

There are many teachings today which have a sound of the truth, and seem good, but are not the gospel. For example, there is a popular teaching that we are potential saints, children of God, and we only need to realize it to live above ourselves by the power of positive thinking. It all looks so right and plausible. It certainly is a bad thing to have a deep sense of inferiority, but confession of sin and true salvation are a glorious and effective remedy, giving the heart the assurance that one is a son of God. There is no short cut. We must repent at the foot of the cross in lowliness of heart before we can rise in new life. Discernment will differentiate between the seemingly good and the real.

Occult Distraction

It is hard to know why the occult receives such major attention from Christian people. In some areas, of course — in Africa, especially — demons are a daily reality; there I find myself on a major battleground. Usually the enemy works on a far broader front than that, however, not merely in the one sector of physical manifestations. We should learn from Paul, as we pointed out earlier. He did nothing about a possessed person until the situation demanded it. Demon hunting is something for which there is, notably, no apostolic example. But it fascinates some, to the exclusion of tackling the common evils of depravity and unbelief in the human heart and preaching the gospel. Ironically, they neglect the Word of God which is the sword of the Spirit and the only offensive weapon Paul mentions in our armory in Ephesians 6. I heard my friend Ray McCauley say, "Some people are more demon- conscious than Jesus-conscious."

Smith Wigglesworth always preached about faith in God, but there are "experts" now teaching only about demons; there are even schools that train in the lore of demonology instead of the whole counsel of God. They justify their schools on the suspicious grounds that the Bible says little about casting out evil spirits and they have to redress the shortcomings of Scripture and teach from experience. However, 2 Peter 1:3-4 says the "great and precious promises" are everything we need for "life and godliness."

Some extremely dangerous practices can emerge here. Many like to put on their spiritual boxing gloves and, with a fierce and menacing air, stand face-to-face with Satan, with violence, shouting and commanding, maybe for hours. One demonologist told a twenty-four-year-old graduate that she needed the demon to be beaten out of her. She submitted hopefully to this humiliation, but without feeling any improvement. This should never be; it is unhealthy and unedifying, and it directly contradicts the biblical model. Some violent exorcisms have caused death and even criminal prosecution. The press reported cases in London in 1985 and 1994 and another in Australia in 1993. The word of command should be all that is needed in most cases, as we see in New Testament instances of deliverance. Meanwhile, the devil gets on with his real job of deceiving the nations, not merely haunting houses or doing other physical activities.

The work of God most certainly includes the casting out of demons. In our gospel crusades in Africa we find ourselves in areas where the very atmosphere is polluted with demons. Witchcraft abounds. Recently, some demon-possessed men cast spells and danced around my hotel all night. When I have begun to preach and mention the name of Jesus, often scores of demons manifest themselves immediately. Victims begin to writhe, scream and disturb the proclamation of the Word. I do not stop preaching, for that is the strategy of the devil. For the sixty or so manifesting demon possession, 160,000 want to hear the gospel. We have trained workers who are ready to lead the devil-possessed away and deal with them, away from the crowd, while the message of the gospel goes forward. We are not there to put on demonstrations but to preach the gospel.

Some claim to have the gift of discernment, but they use complicated tests and multipage questionnaires, not to mention fearful suggestions to open-minded people. Investigating Spirit-filled believers for such dark powers is surely a poor reflection upon the salvation promises of God. The Holy Spirit makes our bodies His temples and would never come to an agreement with a devil to share such a small apartment or tolerate such a foul and illegal squatter. If our lives are hid with Christ in God, and we have a demon, then it would mean that the demon hid in us is also hid in God! That is unthinkable.

If believers have anything clinging to them, it is the old life, the old man. In that case, Scripture makes us responsible to "put off…the old man…according to the deceitful lusts" and to "put on the new man which was created according to God" (Eph. 4:22-24). No Christian was ever exorcised in Bible times. They were guilty of many sins and weaknesses, but it is never put down to the indwelling of an unclean spirit. The answer to faults was not exorcism, but exercise in godliness, casting off (not out) the unfruitful works of darkness.

Much is made of Christ's words to Peter, "Get behind Me, Satan" (Matt. 16:23). But this was no exorcism, and there was no sign of a demon manifesting or leaving him. After all, Jesus had just said Peter was "blessed," and God had revealed the identity of Jesus to him. Peter could not be blessed of God and have a demon at the same time. But he could say something very human which thrust itself into the heart of Jesus like a dagger of the old temptation in the wilderness.

Judging the Spirits

Where then should we be alert for demon powers? The major area of satanic danger to the church is given us as "doctrines of demons" (1 Tim. 4:1); that is, teachings and innovations thrown into the ring by the enemy. They come from all quarters, religious and secular. Some are subtle half-truths buried in seemingly spiritual or pious expressions. Some may, in fact, be misused scriptures, which is the tact Satan tried out on Jesus in the wilderness. Claims of new revelations have been made which their proponents claim not even the apostles understood! The Scriptures speak of false teachers, false prophets, false Christs, false pastors, false brethren, false guides, lying wonders and wolves in sheep's clothing — not only from outside in the world, but also rising up among believers speaking perverse things.

Satan is behind the things that divide us: the church offshoots; little companies around some leader emphasizing some pet dogma of his own; people majoring on minor matters; groups with issues blown up like balloons by windbag leaders; petty complaints given disproportionate importance. Satan's arrows are errors which open a running wound in the side of the body of Christ, bleeding away the testimony, as the devil planned and as God forewarned us about in the Word. Without the gift of discernment of spirits, the church is weakened and divided everywhere.

Even outside the church, major deceptions will creep into the church itself, as they have already. The enemy's job is to provide intellectual interest for those who do not know the truth but pretend to search for it so they will reject the truth of the gospel. The twentieth century has been marked by the fiasco which brought one of the greatest anti-God movements, Marxist communism, to an end. This movement made war on the church for three-quarters of a century before being recognized as the empty evil it was. God's people everywhere knew it was sinister but they were simply derided as "right wing." No doubt this hydra-headed and anti-God political monster will struggle yet to survive — as does Nazism.

Western thinking has also been dominated by secular and godless theories. Satan has planted agents in the highest educational establishments, even in theological seminaries. Non-Christian or anti-Christian concepts have destroyed the spiritual backbone of nation after nation. My own country of Germany is still recovering from the Bible-doubting cult of intellectualism which was hatched two centuries or so ago with the so-called Enlightenment. It spawned the evils of revolution and war.

The effects have been frightening everywhere. The biblical grounds of morality are being destroyed. Without any inner light, each decade ever since has brought a worse wave of heathenism, evil for evil's sake, destruction and even murder for the sheer pleasure of it, both by governments and devil-inspired individuals. People look for wispy "new political initiatives" because they cannot discern that behind so much of the upheaval in the world is the "prince of the power of the air, the spirit who now works in the sons of disobedience" (Eph. 2:2). The origins of all behavior are moral and spiritual. The believer has a means by which to shun these vastly popular but corrupting trends — the gift of the Spirit of discernment.

For the apostles, the world was full of pagan thought. Paul talked about "the wisdom of this world" (1 Cor. 1:20), thinking particularly of the Greek philosophers who never found God and, after six centuries of acute intellectual activity, were still pagans worshipping at an altar inscribed to "the unknown god" (Acts 17:23). That false wisdom was held in such high worldly esteem (as now) that it was infiltrating and warping Christian teaching. Some tried to merge their mystical or philosophical religious ideas with Christianity. Paul could quote them, but he insisted that they were mutually antagonistic.

In fact, the history of church doctrine has largely been the history of attempts to marry the Christian faith with human secular philosophy — everything from Plato to Berkeley and every other fancy and fashion of thought. The gospel has been constantly hacked, chiseled and molded to fit any and every idea that the devil ever put in human heads. From thousands of churches, certainty has fled. Like ancient cities built on the rubble of previous cities, modern doubt is built upon the discarded theories of the past.

This is what Peter called "damnable heresies" (2 Pet. 2:1). The book of Revelation has a symbol of "three unclean spirits like frogs coming out of the mouth of the dragon, out of the mouth of the beast, and out of the mouth of the false prophet" (Rev. 16:13). They are a trinity of untruth. The Bible does not speak of a few church members being misled only. It speaks about nations, the whole world, heading for Armageddon.

That is where the gift of the discerning of spirits is needed. As believers, we will increasingly find ourselves out of step with society, not "politically correct," because the world is deceived. The gift of discernment will guide us in our walk through dangerous minefields. The Holy Spirit is the Spirit of truth, leading us into all truth, as Jesus promised. The believer is the truth-bearer, and the church is the pillar and ground of the truth.

"Now the Spirit expressly says that in latter times some will depart from the faith, giving heed to deceiving spirits and doctrines of demons" (1 Tim. 4:1). Our first concern is not table rapping, poltergeists or imaginary "green demons" to be coughed up, but the flood of error engulfing the church and the world. Exorcism has an important role in our work for God, but we do not fight demon untruth by exorcism, but by preaching the Word of truth.

Finally, remember again that a gift of discerning of spirits is a manifestation of the Spirit who works as and when needed, just as in a word of wisdom, a word of knowledge or a prophecy. How does it come? In all the ways in which other utterances come: by vision, dream, the Word of God — spontaneous, even unrealized. In short, the Holy Spirit will lead us into all truth, not to make us intellectually great, but to safeguard the mind and soul of God's people. The means by which He sometimes does it is this discerning of spirits.

15

TONGUES AND INTERPRETATION

S tanley H. Frodsham wrote *With Signs Following* in 1946. In this work he quotes stories of people speaking in languages they have never heard or learned. Of course, critics have asserted that it is impossible and have written tongues off with the explanation that they were third- or fourth-hand legends. They would, wouldn't they? These are the same grounds on which the miracles of the Bible are dismissed.

Robert Skinner, as editor of the *Canadian Pentecostal Evangel,* has written about several firsthand instances in *Redemption* magazine, September 1993. His father, fluent in Kiswahili, heard a young woman baptized in the Spirit speaking perfect Kiswahili, which she had never heard in her life and which he translated. His son Gary, whom I personally know, was home from Uganda that year at the Eastern Pentecostal Bible College. A student had a German visitor present who had been a Christian for only two weeks. After the service she expressed her enjoyment and said what a pleasure it had been to hear someone praying in Russian, a language she understood, and also how good the interpretation was. Neither of the two speakers knew any Russian.

Robert Skinner mentions, among other incidents, twenty language students going along skeptically to a Pentecostal meeting and hearing several languages, including fluent Italian and Russian, spoken by people who knew nothing of those languages.

Most of this century it has been impossible to write about tongues except in defense. For those who may still be facing objections and critics, we record something of things said in that long struggle since there will always be contrary views.

Of all the gifts, the gift of tongues has attracted the greatest interest and opposition. The discovery that tongues are a valid Christian experience turned out to be epoch-making for the church. Tongues activated the present worldwide Holy Spirit emphasis and became the catalyst for an evangelistic thrust which has eclipsed everything before it both in enterprise and success.

Speaking with tongues is often given the Greek name *glossolalia*. Because there are various ideas about tongues, their origin and what they are, we will first define what we mean in this book. "Tongues" are earthly or celestial languages spoken only by believers as the Holy Spirit gives them utterance. The speakers may not know what they are saying. Being spiritually empowered, interpretation must be by the same means.

If speaking in tongues takes place in worship, addressed to the whole company, an interpretation must follow. For that reason, it will be easier to consider the two gifts — tongues and interpretation — together for much of this chapter.

203

Tongues in Scripture

There are twenty-six references to tongues in the New Testament: one in Mark 16, four in Acts, and twenty-one in 1 Corinthians. This may seem few considering the weight given to tongues in the modern charismatic-Pentecostal scene. However, references to prophecy often include tongues. On the day of Pentecost when the first disciples spoke with tongues and a vast crowd came together asking what it was all about, Peter explained, "This [speaking with tongues] is what was spoken by the prophet Joel...Your sons and daughters will prophesy" (Acts 2:16-17, NIV). Tongues were prophecy, and if understood by hearers (as on the day of Pentecost) they are as much prophecy as tongues in English would be to English hearers. The same is true, of course, when tongues are followed by an interpretation, as is usual in worship services; they become prophecy.

The *glossolalia* is mentioned in only three books of the entire New Testament, Mark, Acts and 1 Corinthians, but that is not significant. Paul wrote a second letter to the Corinthians and made no reference to tongues or any gift whatever. He also wrote about the Lord's table, the central ordinance of the Christian faith, in a long passage in 1 Corinthians but never gave it a passing mention in the second letter; nor do any other books refer to it except the first three Gospels. Even the Gospel of John says nothing about it, just as it omits a dozen or so other important matters. New Testament writings were prompted by some special need or occasion and not usually to propound a comprehensive theology. Of course, Paul does give us much teaching on particular aspects of the faith, but not right across the whole scale of truth.

Sad Lessons of History

Everyone ought to be given the background to the present operation of tongues in millions of believers. For most of the twentieth century tongues were rejected and even forbidden, despite the command of 1 Corinthians 14:39, "Do not forbid to speak with tongues." Curiously, the statement that "women should keep silent in the churches" (v. 34) was given full weight and applied against women, but the command not to forbid tongues was ignored. There are still churches which silence women and tongues; they show a fine disregard for the whole of chapter 14 except the verse that suits them about women. They also separate that one verse from what Paul says on the same subject elsewhere. In this short chapter, however, we have no space to detail the back-somersault of such theologians.

The tongues people, as they were dubbed, were for decades the traditional targets needing the exhortations to love in 1 Corinthians 13. It is hard for us to see that such critical innuendos displayed much love or that the critics themselves were shining examples of that virtue. Of course, chapter 13 is the Word of God, and we should all take it to heart. It contains nine verses stressing love. But what about the seventy-five verses in this same book which encourage the use of gifts? Indeed, the love chapter itself is about gifts, including tongues (vv. 1,8), and was written to show the attitude in which speaking in tongues should take place. Furthermore, it is followed immediately with the command, "Desire spiritual gifts" (14:1). Unfortunately, the chapter heading destroys the connected thought. Can we give serious attention to the love chapter and ignore the gift of tongues which the love chapter is about?

Those who saw and accepted tongues at the beginning of the twentieth century were some of the most devout and godly Bible-preaching people, products of the Holiness movement itself. They were passionately concerned with world evangelism, and after they accepted the Pentecostal blessing in 1901, a soul-saving revival was soon well on the way which has spanned the century unabated.

The history of the *glossolalia* from the beginning of the first day of the twentieth century is full of spiritual significance. It has produced the greatest soul-saving witness in the entire Christian age. However, the evangelical world conjured up a real fear of tongues, and leaders massed their weight against it. That was tragic, and it had far-reaching consequences. God had sent revival, but it was rejected by millions of Bible-believing Christians. Apostolic-style revival made its own way mainly without evangelical encouragement. When George Jeffreys, the greatest and earliest of British Pentecostal evangelists (the man I mentioned laying hands on me) went through the United Kingdom like a flame of fire, warnings against him went out from almost every church pulpit. In Britain's second largest city, Birmingham, tenthousand people received Christ and one thousand testimonies of healing were received; yet a leading free churchman tried to organize opposition against him.

That position changed only when the era of the charismatic renewal began in the late 1950s and 1960s. The nations which could have been swept by revival if the moving of the Spirit in this new way had been accepted by evangelicals were instead swept by war. This sad rejection of biblical gifts was incomprehensible. Slanderous and false reports were a main reason. The enemy and "accuser of the brethren" (Rev. 12:10) made fear his major strategy. The devil could see what damage a miraculous gospel would do to his infernal kingdom. In fact, the very zeal of the "tongues people" to win others for Christ actually deepened alarm among Bible-believers and also liberals. The most godly leaders were misled by the general reports, prejudice and practical pressures. To accept tongues would have put one of the most eminent evangelicals outside the camp and, no doubt, outside his church.

In 1904 the Welsh revival began. It created almost desperate hunger worldwide for such blessing. In Germany the evangelicals organized conventions and prayer efforts. The cry was, "Lord, do it again." The revival they visualized was a repeat of the Wesley-Whitefield-Finney-Edwards awakenings. But God wanted to do a new thing and waited.

In Germany an evangelical leader with no charismatic experience began experimental services for the baptism in the Spirit which drew a mixed multitude of wonder seekers, many of dubious religious stock. Things were allowed to get out of hand, and two experienced Pentecostal women from Norway who had been brought in to help went home disgusted.

The damage was far-reaching and spawned the infamous Berlin Declaration, which denounced the tongues movement as "from below," or of the devil.[1] This short document was merely assertive and contained not a single argument, scriptural or otherwise. Most German evangelicals had to toe the line it laid down, however, under threat of being disfellowshipped. Thus, the declaration rooted itself deeply and bore bitter fruit.

Today, as I write, praise God, I personally have found a new attitude in Germany and everywhere else among evangelicals toward the Pentecostal/charismatic revival. The leaves of the eighty-year-old declaration are yellowing, and an attitude of Christian love is slowly wiping out past misunderstanding. Perhaps this may be the passing forever of those tragic days.

I think it should also be recorded that, not surprisingly, many within the revival eased their foot off the spiritual accelerator, afraid of persecution. There was a general desire not to offend the mainline church by ostentatious tongues, and often it was thought foolish to mention such a strange practice too publicly. Eventually, the charismatic renewal movement began bringing release from this and other inhibiting cautions.

The Basic Problem

The foregoing will, we hope, help a new generation to understand the background to any lingering hesitations about tongues. There are many who have no objections when others speak in tongues, but they are not interested in it for themselves. Is it possible to be Pentecostal/charismatic without speaking with tongues? Well, on the first truly Pentecostal day they all spoke with tongues. Other supernatural gifts are fine — healing, casting out demons, prophecy, wisdom, knowledge and miracles. But there is a difference: None of these requires quite the same self-surrender. They can operate while we keep our best coat buttoned up in dignity. We can indeed heal the sick, give forth wisdom, knowledge and prophecies all quite majestically, but speaking with tongues is different. We can even receive salvation with propriety, but tongues seem to be a humbling of our dignity and composure. Maybe that is why God gives them!

Many Christians have been brought up with anti-tongues attitudes and have become conditioned against the practice. Others have been disillusioned. Those using artificial methods of inducing tongues have done considerable damage. But at the core is fear, a psychological instinct to hold on to ourselves, whereas to speak with tongues looks too much like losing control. This is a needless fear. God never takes over like that and robs us of our will. "The spirits of the prophets are subject to the prophets" (1 Cor. 14:32).

According to Acts 2:4, "they all...began to speak with other tongues as the Spirit gave them utterance." When the will of man and the will of God come together in balance, then, and then only, utterance is possible. We need not be afraid of being "taken over," and we should never allow it. The baptism in the Spirit is not to be described as being possessed by the Holy Spirit. It is not Spirit-possession. A demon may render people possessed, but not the blessed Spirit of God. We should, of course, recognize that God has a right to us as temples and as His servants. "I beseech you therefore, brethren, by the mercies of God, that you present your bodies a living sacrifice, holy, acceptable to God, which is your reasonable service" (Rom. 12:1).

If we want the Holy Spirit we should remember what Peter says: "Holy men of God spoke as they were moved [carried along] by the Holy Spirit" (2 Pet. 1:21). They had no qualms about it, no worries about being possessed or about keeping their self-possession and dignity. Dignity is not one of the fruits of the Spirit anyway, but joy is! God never wrests control, but He does need to come into the flesh and share in the business of our speech. As for dignity, if we want what the apostles got, they did not stand on their dignity too much. They were mocked and accused of being drunk on the day of Pentecost. But that is a small cost for such a big benefit.

Our real handicap is pure instinct: "I am me, and nobody else is going to get so close to me that anything I do is not completely me. Not even God." We zip our souls up and regard the Holy Spirit as an intruder. He wants to make our bodies His temple. That is the trouble — it is just our bodies that we are so fussy about maintaining inviolate.

The Spirit of God has not come to violate. It is not an invasion; we were made for His indwelling. As has often been said, there is a God-shaped vacuum in our souls. Only God can fill it. That is the crux of the matter. The human heart has a golden gate (like that of Jerusalem) which will never be opened except by the Lord of hosts.

God wants us not only spiritually, but physically. That is the revolution of Pentecost, and that is the Rubicon so many fear to cross while admiring those who have. Physically and in every way we are to be one with Him, we in Him and He in us, like a sponge in water. A cloth in purple dye takes on the character of the element into which it is dipped. So do those baptized in the Spirit.

If He dwells in us physically then, should there not be a physical sign? What else but speaking with tongues? Isn't the tongue a rudder that steers the ship, like James says (3:4-5)? Then what does it mean when we don't let God use our tongues to speak with? If the gift is from Him, if we speak with tongues as the Spirit gives utterance, could it be anything but wonderful?

The glorious experience of being swept into the ocean of God's purposes, carried along (like the prophets of Israel) by that Pentecostal mighty rushing wind — is that what we are afraid of? Has the starch of what we call civilization stiffened our garb and turned into steel armor so that it has become difficult to "put on Christ"? Where are His tears? Where is His passion? Where is our cross-bearing? Where is His total unself-consciousness and yieldedness to God? The world admires every passionate enthusiasm except one — the love for God. What do we want? Our cozy culture and sophistication or the burning and palpitating drive of the divine nature?

It has not yet seemed to have had any wide recognition that the baptism in the Spirit with tongues is a truth which enhances all other truths. A new dimension is opened to us not only in life, but also in theology and every relationship. Truth shines more brilliantly at every turn of the jewel. God is in the flesh, not just spiritually. Joel had said the Spirit would be poured out on all *flesh*. It is a pity that the NIV changes that to *people*. God comes upon us in our flesh as well as our spirit.

Whether we speak about salvation or forgiveness or redemption, the flesh is involved — even when we speak of God, for "the Word became flesh" (John 1:14). There is no way that the divine oneness with our human nature could now be better demonstrated than when the Spirit gives utterance with us. The presence of God in His people has always affected them vocally. Theologians now have to think in terms of what happened at Pentecost or miss the key to an enlarged library of truth. If the only perfect Man who ever lived was a divine-human union, and we are destined to be like Him, why shun any evidence of it in the present day? The fullness of the Godhead indwelt Him bodily.

The Gift of God

The Pentecostals in their little storefront churches and backstreet halls stuck to their guns for half a century of contempt. Those church groups, now numbering 150 million, usually write tongues in their statements of fundamental beliefs as the sign of the baptism in the Spirit. Whatever arguments are used, whether the book of Acts was intended to teach theology or not, the record is enough. The Bible way of being full of the Spirit and knowing it is clear enough. It was always with outward manifestations, and the only one invariably mentioned is tongues. Nobody, but nobody, in apostolic days had it any other way.

If people don't like tongues, how do they propose they will know they have the Holy Spirit? How will it show in their personality? Going around healing others doesn't show how we ourselves are blessed. We are talking about "new creatures"; not old creatures made a little more lively, but life from the dead.

Tongues are the only gift named in every list in 1 Corinthians 12-14. Tongues — real tongues — would be impossible without God. It is a gift from heaven. Should anybody protect and defend themselves against it? In an earlier chapter we said that there is no such thing as greater and lesser gifts. There is also no such thing as a gift of so little consequence that it need not interest us. God does not give trivial gifts. If we cannot see their value, He does.

There are those who teach that we can be filled with the Spirit without tongues or even that we receive the Spirit at new birth and seek the gifts afterward. It eliminates the need for the Pentecostal "initial evidence" of tongues. Well, why is such teaching so welcome? No tongues — what attraction is that? If you don't bother with this gift, another will have to be crossed off the Corinthian list — interpretation. Are we superior to what God offers?

Tongues in Operation

Literature on tongues would fill a library. In this book we are attempting to set down guidance, understanding and something more. The object is to stimulate the desire for the God-given gifts which have always proved to come hand-in-hand with faith and evangelistic vision.

The tongues people are becoming a major factor in history, secular and religious, simply because of their eagerness to see others turn to God. There is a bright fire in their souls, a conviction that runs deep. Don't ask how or why. It is there. Perhaps others have it too, but certainly millions would not have it at all unless speaking with tongues had introduced the indwelling Spirit to them.

Earlier we referred to the fact that the nine manifestations which Paul describes in the first list of 1 Corinthians 12 are not all there are. This is a quick list of gifts which particularly affect Christian worship. Other works of the Spirit, such as casting out demons, taking up serpents and immunity to poison, are not part of normal worship.

Paul ranks prophecy higher than the Corinthians did, who preferred the more showy manifestations, especially tongues. The love of the sensational is not unknown in any age, and it is evident enough today. The miraculous may be sought purely because it is sensational. Speaking with tongues in Corinth sounded to Paul like "sounding brass or clanging cymbal" (1 Cor. 13:1) — sounding off, showing off. Paul suddenly reduces this proud accomplishment to dependency on a prophesier, saying a tongues man is not to speak at all without an interpretation.

Interpretation

The word used for interpretation in 1 Corinthians 12:10 is *hermeneia*. The experts tell us that this means "to explain what is said" rather than to translate. In 14:27-28 it is similar: "to put into words" *(diermeneueto)*.

We would like to offer some help and guidelines, especially as tongues used publicly is expected to be in the context of worship.

What may be concisely expressed by the Spirit in one language may need more explaining in English. We know nothing about the tongues of angels, which could be much more concise than our languages, needing many earth-language words to interpret them. A brief utterance in tongues, followed by an interpretation five times as long, may have another explanation, namely a prophetic development of the same theme continuing in the spirit of prophecy.

The interpretation does not need to take place immediately after the tongues speaker has ceased. The whole service does not need to be quieted waiting for the interpreter to begin. There is no reason why it should not be given later. For that matter it could even be given in a subsequent meeting if the Spirit allows it and the same congregation is present, though that would be rare.

It has been said that some utterances in tongues are only praise to God and need no interpretation. But why not interpret praise? Tongues and interpretation have a worship quality, and praise is edifying. Those who understood the languages spoken on the day of Pentecost heard them "speaking...the wonderful works of God" (Acts 2:11). That is like the Psalms. Why not now?

The wonderful works of God before Christ were described in

the Psalms as His miracle acts, such as the deliverance from Egypt. Worship should not be mainly about bowing before a heavenly (and unimaginable) throne in heaven. The wonderful work of God was that God was in Christ reconciling the world unto Himself. Calvary has always been the Christian theme. So when speaking with tongues is interpreted, the great salvation spoken of by the prophets will not surprisingly be the theme of modern prophets. The glory of the cross and supreme work of God written in blood at Calvary were the subject of praise in glory when John saw what was going on there (Rev. 5).

To say that Paul discourages tongues is one of the most remarkable instances of turning Scripture on its head that I have ever known. 1 Corinthians 14 makes statements about tongues which are not even made about prophecy. "He who speaks in a tongue does not speak to men but to God" (v. 2). "In the spirit he speaks mysteries" (v. 2). "If I pray in a tongue, my spirit prays" (v. 14). "Tongues are for a sign...to unbelievers" (v. 22). "You are praising God with your spirit" (v. 16, NIV).

Service Order

The Corinthian instructions end with verses 39 and 40 of chapter 14: "Therefore, brethren, desire earnestly to prophesy, and do not forbid to speak with tongues. Let all things be done decently and in order." What order? Ours or God's? Our cast-iron structured proceedings? That is not indicated at all. God's order may have an alpine ruggedness about it and still retain an aspect of grandeur. Worship can have spontaneity, the mountain a surprise view. "Whenever you come together, each of you has a psalm, has a teaching, has a tongue, has a revelation, has an interpretation" (v. 26). This is Holy Spirit worship — rivers of living water, streams in the desert.

However, speaking with tongues is not confined to use in church. Paul wishes that they all spoke with tongues. Obviously not everybody could give an utterance when gathered for worship (compare 14:5,23). There would not be time unless they stayed a week. Paul's wish for all to speak with tongues could only be realized if people exercised their fluency in private worship.

Speaking in tongues is prayer (14:22) and is therefore one way in which to "pray in the Spirit," especially when "we do not know what we should pray for," as Romans 8:26 says. It is interesting that this applies not necessarily to praying for someone else but also for ourselves, for it continues, "the Spirit Himself makes intercession for us." We pray for ourselves when we pray in tongues. This explains why millions find themselves "getting through" when the mood seems to be missing in prayer if they take advantage of this manifestation in their lives. But Paul is mainly concerned with tongues in public worship.

It is in the church that Paul visualizes the operation of the gifts for "edification and exhortation and comfort" (14:3), and any prophecy should be proved by others. These two instructions make it very clear that tongues, interpretation and prophecy are not for private guidance, nor for the family circle, nor between friends, nor between husband and wife. This kind of thing should take place in the congregation where there are others to judge.

Experience has shown how important this is. The practice of using tongues and interpretation privately in the home, more particularly to obtain guidance, is not merely inadvisable — it has brought calamity and shipwreck. It is a way to divide churches. There must be others to judge, which means that oversight is needed even in church worship.

What Are Tongues?

Tongues have been explained as psychological, being "thrown up from the subconscious mind under mental stress." It amazes me that such fantastic abilities are attributed to the subconscious mind — that people can utter lengthy and intelligible speeches in languages they have never heard, and even describe in tongues matters completely outside their knowledge.

Nils Bloch Hoel's *The Pentecostal Movement* (1964) diagnoses tongues-speaking as a psychological illness and tongues-speakers as a subspecies. His medical opinion is that "real xenolalia" (foreign languages) is some sort of mental lapse, when long-forgotten foreign phrases are released in "motoric speech" when the patient is in a state of ecstasy or trauma. He wraps this farfetched nonsense around with high-sounding jargon: "hypermnesia" or "cryptonesia," and considers that a "satisfactory rational explanation." Nothing could be less "satisfactory" or "rational."

Those of us who speak with tongues daily can state that it is not done in an ecstasy or trauma, and that we are in full control of our mental state. Nils Bloch Hoel, however, is himself not so sure he has explained things, for he adds that future investigation in psychology may come forward with some different explanation. Indeed, yes — the Holy Spirit perhaps? Why not? And that is an explanation nobody can disprove.

By way of answer we can mention another Norwegian, Thoralf Gilbrant, a scholar and international editor of the sixteen-volume *Biblical Library*. In 1985, at the Pentecostal World Conference, he testified that his grandmother had preached to Italian ship crews in fluent Italian, not knowing a word of it. He himself heard an elderly choir man praying in beautiful British English, not American. Later, assuming the man had lived here, he struck up a conversation with him and discovered he knew no English whatsoever. The choir man was not in a state of ecstasy, trauma or anything approaching it.

Others think that it was a very special, one-time miracle on the day of Pentecost when the 120 spoke with recognizable languages which they had never learned and that the tongues in Corinth were quite different. There is not only no evidence whatsoever for such an idea but no value in the idea either, except to push back the miraculous into remote history.

An objection has been raised that tongues have been heard among those who are not Christians. Mormons can produce their own cases of tongues. No doubt. In fact, as referred to earlier, the oracles at the temples of pagan gods sometimes gave forth their pronouncements in gibberish through the lips of vestal virgins, which priests purported to interpret. The devil, like the magicians of Egypt, can counterfeit the miracles of God and supernaturally impart utterances. That is anticipated by Paul in 1 Corinthians 12:3: "No one speaking by the Spirit of God calls Jesus accursed." Paul was not inventing a hypothetical possibility. It could happen and possibly did, but it would be by another spirit other than from God. The occult is supernatural as well as the gifts of the Spirit.

That Satan can produce phenomena does not mean it is all satanic. Jesus was meeting such a fear when He said, "If a son asks for bread from any father among you, will he give him a stone? Or if he asks for a fish, will he give him a serpent instead of a fish? Or if he asks for an egg, will he offer him a scorpion? If you then, being evil, know how to give good gifts to your children, how much more will your heavenly Father give the Holy Spirit to those who ask Him?" (Luke 11:11-13). Speaking with tongues has sometimes been more baffling to unbelief and more convincing to the unprejudiced than healing and visible miracles.

The question of what the gift of tongues is can now be easily answered. Not everybody who speaks with tongues is gifted for their use in public worship — which Paul is concerned with in 1 Corinthians. If certain people in a church seem to be prominent in this utterance, that is how it should be. *Gift* has more than one meaning. Speaking with tongues is a gift of God in the general sense, but in the church sense the gift has come to the man or woman who frequently feels a special inspiration to edify the congregation in this way — with an interpreter, fulfilling the law "out of the mouth of two witnesses."

Tongues That Aid Us

Let us now enumerate the ways in which we are helped by speaking with tongues:

- They are an utterance in prayer for needs we cannot express and don't know how to pray. They enable us to sense the presence of God and that He is inclining His ear to hear us.
- Demon hindrance is overcome.
- When our minds can no longer concentrate, our spirit prays.
- We can pray in tongues when we are otherwise having to concentrate upon some mechanical task, such as driving a car.
- We edify ourselves.

We leave this important subject at this juncture, though it deserves far more examination. The Spirit of God is seeking every way to break through into our needy lives and our desperate world. May we be open to His partnership!

Postscript

SOME ANALOGIES

Now that we have been able to dig beneath the surface of those gift references in 1 Corinthians, I would like us to relax and indulge ourselves in the Bible picture gallery of things that have been.

The Divine Dowry

Carrying a fortune, Eliezer the Damascene, chief steward of a wealthy estate, journeyed from Kiriath-arba to distant Aram Naharaim. He sought a bride, but not for himself. A chaste virgin was needed for the son of the household. Ready for when she was found, Eliezer carried rich gifts from the father to adorn her. Then

Eliezer would bring her back for the marriage. Eliezer had once been heir to the whole estate, but when a son had been born, his interests were entirely concerned with the natural heir.

Eventually, his road led him to Rebekah, a lovely and intelligent girl. She proved willing to share the life of a man she had never seen, Isaac, the only son of Abraham. Eliezer covered her in the golden treasures and immediately began the return journey to Kiriath-arba.

It took many weary days, but at last the journey ended, and Rebekah was presented to Isaac. He saw her veiled, but he recognized the jewelry she wore, the gifts his father had chosen. This was his bride (Gen. 24).

This ancient cameo reflects the greatest story ever told. The Father has sent the Holy Spirit, servant-Spirit, seeking a chaste bride for His Son. It is by the Spirit of God that we are drawn to Christ "whom having not seen you love" (1 Pet. 1:8). The Spirit does not speak of Himself but of the Son. He is the Paraclete — "one who walks beside" — who accompanies the bride on the weary journey of life until she joins the heavenly bridegroom as He comes to meet her. The servant-Spirit also has gifts to bestow.

A hundred Bible passages speak of it; in fact, the whole Bible. It seems that the Father loves the Son. He could scarcely conceal it even though the true character of the Godhead was not fully disclosed. In many a human episode (included by His inspiration in the Scriptures) there are hints of this great secret, His love for His only Son, until finally the Father announced to the world: "You are my beloved Son; in You I am well pleased" (Luke 3:22). There was a further revelation — a bride was sought for that Son. Paul spoke of it. "This is a great mystery, but I speak concerning Christ and the church" (Eph. 5:32).

There is no mystery in earthly marriage, but there is awesome wonder in the bride sought for the heavenly bridegroom. "I promised you to one husband, to Christ, so that I might present you as a pure virgin to him" (2 Cor. 11:2, NIV).

The Bridegroom Comes

The bride, the church, has been endowed with the many and varied gifts of God. The Holy Spirit Himself is described as one of them — the one who walks with us as Jesus once walked with His disciples, a personal and holy companion (Acts 1:4-5). There are countless more gifts: "Praise be to the God and Father of our Lord Jesus Christ, who has blessed us in the heavenly realms with every spiritual blessing in Christ...to the praise of his glorious grace, which he has freely given us in the One he loves. In him we have redemption through his blood, the forgiveness of sins, in accordance with the riches of God's grace that he lavished on us with all wisdom and understanding...Christ loved the church and gave himself up for her" (Eph. 1:3, 6-8, NIV; 5:25, NIV).

His love, and indeed everything we receive from God, are all *charismata*, favors, unlimited and unmerited. Grace (*charis*) itself is a *charisma*, a love gift. Then come the gifts of the Spirit, adorning the church as Rebekah was once beautified by the rings upon her ears, ankles and arms, and by the tiara upon her head, "a bride adorned for her husband" (Rev. 21:2). The most conspicuous event today in the church universally is the ready acceptance of the gifts of the Spirit. The Spirit of God is moving today in supernatural greatness, touching the lives of perhaps one in every ten people in the world.

This adorning of the bride itself holds a wonderful significance. When Rebekah accepted the gifts from Eliezer, it meant that soon she would meet Isaac and become his bride. Is that the real meaning today as we see the Spirit bestowing His gifts upon the church? Is the bride now being prepared to meet the bridegroom? Is the marriage of the Lamb at hand? Is that day, known only to the

Father, near? The bride is still veiled. The world cannot see her face as she really is, but the cry is being heard, "Behold, the bridegroom is coming" (Matt. 25:6).The church is wearing the Father's gifts, and we have the "living hope" of the coming of Christ. "Everyone who has this hope in Him purifies himself" (1 John 3:3).

There is another lovely detail in the story of Isaac and Rebekah. He came out "in the field," and there he first met her (Gen. 24:63-65). "The field is the world" (Matt. 13:38), and the promise of Christ is that He will come back here for His bride, into this world, once the field of His labors and suffering, at the end of her long centuries of journeying. "The Lord Himself will descend from heaven…the dead in Christ will rise…Then we who are alive and remain shall be caught up together with them in the clouds to meet the Lord in the air. And thus we shall always be with the Lord" (1 Thess. 4:16-17). "Even so, come, Lord Jesus!" (Rev. 22:20).

The Golden Bells

Christ is not only the bridegroom, but also "our great high priest" (see Heb. 8:6-12; 10:21). Every year the high priest of Israel went through the second veil of the temple (there were no doors) into the holy of holies. There he sprinkled the blood of the atonement before the Lord. Would he be accepted on behalf of Israel?

The assembled men of Israel did not see him enter the holiest place, but they heard him. The hem of his robes was decorated with golden bells. When he moved they were heard, until he passed into the holy of holies. Then the heavy temple hangings folded behind him, and the sound of the bells could not be heard outside. The worshippers waited anxiously to hear. The bells would assure them that their priest had not died in judgment, but had been accepted by God. The bells were heard when the priest went into God's presence and a second time when he came out again.

We read, "[Christ] entered heaven itself...to appear for us in God's presence...once for all at the end of the ages" (Heb. 9:24, 26, NIV). At that time sounds were heard — not bells, but "a mighty rushing wind" from heaven and the praising tongues of Pentecost. The people said, "We hear them speaking in our own tongues the wonderful works of God" (Acts 2:11).

The centuries passed, and the heavenly sounds were scarcely heard. Today, there is a sound from heaven again. The wind of the Spirit blows mightily, and men and women worldwide again prophesy and speak with tongues. Is "the High Priest of our confession" already beginning to move through the second veil, and then through the first veil so that "every eye shall see Him, and they also who pierced Him" (Rev. 1:7, KJV)? The Scripture says, "He will appear a second time...to bring salvation for those who are waiting for him" (Heb. 9:28, NIV).

Then the gifts will cease, the need at an end. That is what we read in 1 Corinthians 13:8, 10: "Love never fails...Prophecies... will cease...tongues...will be stilled...knowledge...will pass away...but when perfection comes, the imperfect disappears" (NIV). "The perfect" is the perfect day, when He comes.

Some look for a scripture to support their teaching that the gifts were withdrawn when the apostles died. They have tied this teaching to one single verse, the verse just quoted which says the gifts would cease when "that which is perfect has come." Quite gratuitously they invented the idea that "the perfect" was the finished New Testament, the completion of the canon, and that would bring about the end of tongues and prophecies. But if Paul meant the New Testament canon, it certainly didn't enter the Corinthians' heads. It never entered Paul's head either, for the whole concept of a New Testament was certainly never visualized in those early years. In fact, it was not settled until the fourth century A.D. when the great Bishop Athanasius sent out a cyclical letter, and quite incidentally listed the twenty-seven New Testament books. What everybody did understand was that "the perfect" would only come when Christ returned.

The perfect state lies ahead of us still, as we await the coming of the bridegroom and the return through the veil of the great high priest. Love will then continue, we shall see face-to-face, not a reflection in a mirror, and we will know as we are known.

Analogy and Reality

The gifts are love tokens, like Rebekah's jewelry. They declare our heavenly Lover's serious intentions to take us to Himself. They are the "earnest" of things to come: "Now it is God who makes both us and you stand firm in Christ. He anointed us...and put his Spirit in our hearts as a deposit, guaranteeing what is to come" (2 Cor. 1:21-22, NIV).

The Eliezer story is a picture for me of an unforgettable occasion — my first stadium crusade. God put ten thousand people before me. Many were drawn by the Holy Spirit to receive Christ into their lives. Many were also healed. Then the Lord whispered to me that He had the gift of the Holy Spirit for them.

I explained it to the people, and we prayed. It was like putting a key into the doors of the treasure house of heaven and opening them. Before my astonished gaze, within seconds, hundreds upon hundreds "spoke with tongues and prophesied as the Spirit gave them utterance." I had seen the servant-Spirit that day wooing the bride. Now I saw Him adorning her, these precious people, with the Father's bridal gifts.

The Lover or His Gifts?

For Rebekah, the excitement was not merely the glittering

bracelets or finger rings, but the waiting bridegroom whose face she had never seen. Drawing nearer to her future home in the care of Eliezer she scanned the road ahead for her first glimpse of Isaac. She was not absorbed in admiring her gifts.

Signs and wonders are absorbing Christian attention everywhere. Unfortunately, for some, the phenomena of the Spirit can be the be-all and end-all of faith. Providing something marvelous happens, that is the object. A writer spoke of a typical wanderer from church to church, who is saying something like this: "I am looking for a prophetic church that has power over demons; has cleared the sky above it of the satanic umbrella; that sees ambulances return empty from the services; where the pastor has discernment; which is structured with the five-fold organizational gifts; that gives an opportunity for words from the Lord without quenching the Spirit; that recognizes the power of praise; that claims prosperity and success; and where the gifts of the Spirit are in full operation."

All of what he suggested is very good, of course, but what about looking for a church that expounds the Word and where the eternal theme of Christ's redemption rings the bells of joy and hope? What about a church where the love of Jesus is the big thing, and the songs are filled with truth and salvation? Gifts dare not be a treasure above Jesus the Giver! "To those who eagerly wait for Him He will appear a second time" (Heb. 9:28).

> The bride eyes not her garment,
> But her dear bridegroom's face,
> I will not gaze at glory, but on my King of grace;
> Not at the crown He gifteth, but on His pierced hand.
> The Lamb is all the glory of Immanuel's land.[1]

In Africa I find preachers who often have only one message —

physical healing. I believe my own calling is primarily to present the simple gospel of salvation. Jesus saves from sin. Then the power of God is always present to heal.

The spiritually hungry are fed by the Word of God and not by healings, as wonderful and necessary as the latter are. These precious souls are moved as I tell them about the love of Jesus. When people respond to the gospel — often in many thousands — then the servant-Spirit of God has begun His work. He has won them for God's Isaac, our Lord Jesus. Afterward comes His dowry — right there as we look across a sea of heads in some vast concourse, gifts given to hundreds of thousands of new believers.

Paul said, "I speak with tongues more than you all" (1 Cor. 14:18), and he wrote, "Earnestly desire the *charismata*" (1 Cor. 12:31). But his own outlook was dominated by something else. He wrote, "[That you] may be able to comprehend with all saints what is the width and length and depth and height — to know the love of Christ which passes knowledge; that you may be filled with all the fullness of God" (Eph. 3:18-19).

"All the fullness of God" is nothing less than His love. Thinking of Rebekah's dowry gifts, an expert might evaluate them in cash terms, but she knew their real worth. They were the treasure of love. The gifts are tokens of something greater than themselves, more than miracle and wonder powers. We receive them as the tokens of the love of Christ. The gifts are intended to strengthen our attachment to one another and to Him. There are seventy-one verses on the gifts in chapters 12 and 14 of 1 Corinthians, but they are warmed by the fires of love in the thirteen verses of chapter 13.

It is a heartbreaking error to forget the Giver. Christ warns us that some will come to Him "on that day" and will claim that they cast out devils, prophesied and did many mighty works in Christ's name, but His sad response will be "I never knew you. Away from me, you evildoers!" (Matt. 7:22-23, NIV). We have written this book to focus attention on and create a desire for the gifts, and to encourage everyone to see the Holy Spirit manifesting His powers throughout the world. Let me say, however, that it is a means to an end; that directly or indirectly, people will turn to Christ to serve and love Him.

Ten times in the first ten verses of 1 Corinthians Paul names the name of Jesus. Like Bernard of Clairvaux, one of the most influential religious figures in Europe in the mid-twelfth century, who wrote "Jesus, the very thought of Thee, with sweetness fills my breast...Jesus, our only joy be Thou, as Thou our prize will be...Jesus, be thou our glory now, and through Eternity." Perhaps the most moving verse in all the writings of Paul is Galatians 2:20: "It is no longer I who live, but Christ lives in me; and the life which I now live in the flesh I live by faith in the Son of God, who loved me and gave Himself for me."

"Desire spiritual gifts," said Paul in 1 Corinthians 14:1, but for himself he cherished a greater desire — "I also count all things but loss for the excellence of the knowledge of Christ Jesus my Lord...that I may know Him" (Phil. 3:8, 10). He reminded the gift-conscious Corinthians that they were "called into the fellowship of [God's] Son, Jesus Christ our Lord" (1 Cor. 1:9). That is the ultimate object of all the Spirit's gifts.

The Golden Lampstand

The Roman Catholic theologian Hans Küng said, "To rediscover the *charismata* is to rediscover the ecclesiology of Saint Paul." In everyday language, the gifts have everything to do with what Paul says about the church. Another analogy of the church is found in Revelation 1:12, 20. Jesus is seen standing amid the seven churches of Asia which are represented by golden lampstands.

The temple lampstand of seven lamps was beaten out of one

talent of gold. It had a fuel source in the central shaft and base (see Zech. 4:2-3). The single oil source speaks of the "one Spirit," the Holy Spirit. The seven lamps (see also Rev. 4:5) are a symbol of perfection, just as in Revelation 5:6 seven horns signify perfect power, seven eyes (Rev. 5:6; Zech. 3:9) perfect knowledge, and seven Spirits of God signify the perfect personality of the Holy Spirit. The Holy Spirit and the church are joined.

That is the Spirit by which the church fulfils its entire purpose. A lamp has only one function, to give light. Without the Holy Spirit, the lamp of God's people, described by Jesus as "the light of the world," becomes lightless. In fact, the foundation of the church is maintained by the Spirit only, and its fabric crumbles without the Spirit. The sticking plaster of ecumenism or organization cannot prevent it eventually becoming no more than a tourist attraction of things that once were — a beautiful ruin.

The Breastplate

Another picture comes from the breastplate of the high priest of Israel. It displayed twelve gems set in gold, each bearing the names of a tribe of Israel. The priest wore it over his heart as he went into the inner sanctuary, the holy of holies. That place had no window nor any lamp. The priest carried no light and no naked fire. The glow of his incense was clouded in the smoke arising from it. There was a light there, however. It was said that the "shekinah," or visible glory, lit the holy of holies from beneath the wings of the cherubim over the ark of the covenant.

This glory was reflected in the jewels in the high priest's breastplate. Splashes of prismatic color would cross the curtain walls reflecting only the glory of God. It is a perfect picture. We have no glory of our own, however gem-like our shining personal talents. The only true light comes from Christ. We are witnesses to that light as we turn our faces to Him and reflect what Jesus was and is. Unless we catch that light in our own lives, nobody will see it. The gifts of the Spirit are His gifts; they are not our natural talents or graces.

Whatever we can do, whatever we can be, whatever we should do, whether by natural or supernatural abilities, the Spirit of God must burn and shine in it all, that there may be glory in the church by Christ Jesus.

For thine is the kingdom, and the power, and the glory, forever. Amen!

Notes

Chapter 2 – God Has Taken the Field

1 Quoted by Ronald Foulkes in *The Flame Shall Not Be Quenched*, p. 100.

2 Ibid.

3. John Wesley, *Notes on the New Testament*, as quoted by Ronald Foulkes in *The Flame Shall Not Be Quenched*, p. 18.

4. As quoted by John Wesley in his *Works*, volume 13, p. 449: "Sir, the pretending to extraordinary revelations and gifts of the Holy Ghost is a horrid thing, a very horrid thing."

5. Quoted by Foulkes in *The Flame Shall Not be Quenched*.

6. William Shakespeare, *The Merchant of Venice*, act 1, scene 1. Gratiano: "Why should a man, whose blood is warm within, sit like his grandsire cut in alabaster?"

7. Historical baptismal liturgies invariably show that the "chrism" of anointing with oil for the reception of the Spirit did not take place until after baptism, signifying the washing away of sins and the candidate becoming regenerate; that is, post-conversion. See Harold Hunter, *Spirit-Baptism: A Pentecostal Alternative* (Lanham, Md.: University Press of America).

8. D. Martyn Lloyd-Jones, *Joy Unspeakable* (Wheaton, Ill.: Harold Shaw, 1985, reprinted).

Chapter 3 – The Anointing

1. Donald Guthrie, ed., *New Bible Commentary* (Grand Rapids, Mich.: Wm. B. Eerdmans, 1950), s.v. "ointment."
2. Examples of initial reactions to the tongues phenomenon can be found in *The Tongues Baptism* by F.W. Pitt and *The Early Years of the Tongues Movement* by G.H. Lang.
3. Words by D.M. Shanks, from the hymn "He Abides."
4. Words by Samuel Crossman, from the hymn "My Song Is Love Unknown."

Chapter 4 – How the Gifts Came

1. Charles Wesley, "Jesus, the Name High Over All."

Chapter 5 – Golden Rules of the Gifts

1. Margaret Polomo, *Assemblies of God at the Crossroads* (Knoxville: University of Tennessee Press, 1989).
2. These facts are gathered from *Redemption* magazine, June, July and September 1993, and the Church of God *Evangel.*
3. Words by Frederick W. Faber, from the hymn "Souls of Men!"
4. "A Pauline Theology of Charismata," Ph. D. dissertation by Siegfried Schatzmann, lecturer in New Testament Greek and director of studies at Elim Bible College, Nankwich, U.K.
5. Elizabeth Stuart, "Love is...Paul," *Expository Times* 102, no. 9: 264-66.

Chapter 6 – Words of the Word

1. Colin Brown, gen. ed. *Dictionary of New Testament Theology* (Grand Rapids, Mich.: Zondervan Publishing House, 1986), vol. 2, s.v. "*Doron.*"

Chapter 7 – A Word of Wisdom

1. William L. Holladay, ed., *A Concise Hebrew and Aramaic Lexicon of the Old Testament* (Leiden: E.J. Brill, and Grand Rapids, Michigan: William B. Eerdmans Publishing Company, 1988), p. 76.

Chapter 9 – Faith

1. William Wordsworth, *The Excursion*, part 4, line 1293.

Chapter 11 – Healing, Part 2

1. From the essay *Possible Worlds*, 1927.

Chapter 12 – Miracles

1. George Wigram and Ralph Winter, eds., *Word Study Concordance* (Wheaton, Ill.: Tyndale House Publishers, 1979).
2. Words by L.E. Jones, from the hymn "There's Power in the Blood."

Chapter 13 – Prophecy

1. James Dunn, *Jesus and the Spirit* (Belleville, Mich.: Westminster/John Knox Press, 1979).
2. Stanley Burgess, Gary McGee and Patrick Alexander, eds., *Dictionary of Pentecostal and Charismatic Movements* (Grand Rapids, Michigan: Zondervan Publishing House, 1988), s.v., *"Glossolalia,"* by R.P. Spittler, p. 336.

Chapter 14 – Discernment

1. Ralph P. Martin, *The Spirit and the Congregation*, p. 14.

Chapter 15 – Tongues and Interpretation

1. "*Die Berliner Erklärung*" was issued in 1909 by fifty-six evangelical (Pietist-Holiness) leaders following serious mishaps and mishandling of initial Pentecostal meetings in Germany. It had a traumatic and deadening effect upon reception of the Pentecostal movement among evangelicals in Germany. Only within the last year or two has a softening of this attitude been seen, particularly to Reinhold Bonnke.

Postscript — Some Analogies

1. Words by Anne R. Cousins, from the hymn *The Sands of Time Are Sinking*, verse 5.

Other Books by Reinhard Bonnke

Evangelism by Fire
The Assurance of Salvation
The Secret of the Blood of Jesus
How to Receive a Miracle from God
The Baptism in the Holy Spirit
Now That You Are Saved
The Ultimate Plus
Explosion of Life

For more information you may contact:

Reinhard Bonnke Ministries, Inc.
P.O. Box 277440
Sacramento, CA 95827
1-800-HE-HEALS
1-800-434-3257

Ministry Profile

The vision of a blood-washed Africa—a continent washed in the blood of Jesus Christ — propels the ministry of Reinhard Bonnke, founder and director of Christ for all Nations (CfaN).

As a young missionary in Lesotho, Reinhard Bonnke was deeply moved by the great spiritual need for the gospel throughout the continent of Africa. In 1972 Bonnke experienced a recurring vision for several nights. He saw Africa washed in the blood of Jesus and heard the Holy Spirit whisper, "Africa shall be saved." Since then Bonnke has dedicated his life to spreading the gospel from Cape Town to Cairo.

Under the guidance of the Holy Spirit, Bonnke and the CfaN team reached increasingly large numbers of people through his outreach meetings. In 1984 the team began using the world's largest mobile tent—seating thirty-four thousand people. But the attendance at campaign meetings soon far exceeded the capacity of any tent. In 1990 a record-breaking attendance of five hundred thousand people was recorded at a single meeting in Kaduna, Nigeria. Since that time the attendance at many campaign meetings has exceeded one million people.

Reinhard Bonnke has preached to an estimated eight million people in twelve months, probably reaching more people than any other evangelist alive today. Thousands of individuals experience the baptism of the Holy Spirit and miracles of healing at each CfaN campaign. Bonnke welcomes such ministry as confirmation of God's Word for Africa.

Bonnke now affirms that "Africa is being saved," not by might, nor by power—but by the Spirit of God.

In 1994 Bonnke birthed another evangelistic project—taking the message of salvation through Jesus Christ to every household in Europe and beyond. An attractive booklet, *From Minus to Plus,* presents the gospel message. The first distribution reached twenty-five million households throughout the United Kingdom and Ireland, and follow-up is being carried out for all respondents. In 1995 the project will reach out to forty million households in Germany, Austria and Switzerland.

The international headquarters of Christ for all Nations is located in Frankfurt, Germany. Regional offices have been established in Africa, Great Britain, Norway and the United States of America. While Africa remains the primary focus of the ministry, campaigns have been held in countries throughout the world. Many more people are reached through the CfaN video and audio tape ministry.

For further information about the CfaN ministry, please contact:

Reinhard Bonnke Ministries, Inc.
P.O. Box 277440
Sacramento, CA 95827

Other material by Reinhard Bonnke

Africa Shall Be Saved
VHS / 30 Minutes

The power of God is clearly demonstrated in this dramatic video documenting the Tamale crusade. In a city that is said to be 80% Muslim, the Gospel triumphs over the forces of Islam.

The Overcomers
VHS / 60 Minutes

Are you a "hallelujah person"? In this video, Reinhard Bonnke examines the role of an overcomer and, drawing on scriptures from Revelation 3 and 19, explains how you can experience a little heaven on earth.

Intercession: The Detonator
VHS / 60 Minutes

Is your prayer life timid and ineffectual? In this specially recorded Bible study, Reinhard Bonnke shares his insight and experiences of seeking answers to prayer. His own "formula for success" is expressed in a preface to his "dynamite" teaching: "Evangelism without intercession is an explosive without a detonator!"

These and other titles available from:
Reinhard Bonnke Ministries • P.O. Box 277440 • Sacramento, CA 95827

Also available from Reinhard Bonnke

Evangelism by Fire

Twenty power-packed chapters that will challenge you and ignite a fire within your Spirit as Reinhard Bonnke shares his experiences and his insights.

After spending years using "tried and true" methods of evangelism, Reinhard Bonnke yearned to see a new dimension in *Spirit-led* evangelism. Today he sees nations shaken by the power of the Gospel.